Dynamic Supervision

Dynamic Supervision

Problems and Opportunities

Maxine H. Bishop

American Management Association, Inc.

Standard book number: 8144-5197-7

Library of Congress catalog card number: 79-93787

First printing

To
the memory of
Roy

Preface

SUPERVISION IS AN ESSENTIAL AND PERVASIVE function, engaging the time and energies of thousands of individuals in all occupations and professions. It is a complex and often difficult function. Supervisors always must balance the needs of production with the human needs of their employees, and they must balance the objectives of management with the interests and goals of their subordinates. They must acquire a whole new body of skills and knowledge, in addition to the expertise required by their particular occupation or profession. Moreover, the rapid technological and social changes of our modern world have demanded of the supervisor a flexibility and capacity for growth that are unprecedented.

Despite its importance, complexity, and difficulty, supervision is often thrust upon individuals who have not been prepared for it by training or education. They often have no way of anticipating the great variety of problems they will be called upon to resolve or the situations and challenges that will confront them. They have to learn the craft of supervision by trial and error. And they have to make decisions with little to guide them besides common sense. If they attend supervisory training courses, they are likely to acquire from them only a fraction of the specialized knowledge they need.

This book was written for both the new and the experienced supervisor. It attempts to give a broad and penetrating picture of the total supervisory responsibility and to identify the particular abilities a supervisor should have in order to be effective. It gives equal weight to conceptual skills and to interpersonal skills. Both are essential. It is not a how-to-do-it book because good supervision cannot be practiced by learning rote responses or techniques. Supervision is a creative process, and the best supervisors are those with understanding, perception, judgment, and imagination.

The concepts and principles presented here are related to everyday work situations by means of numerous anecdotes and illustrations. A certain amount of theory is introduced, and major research studies in motivation are described. Some knowledge of the behavioral science literature should enable the supervisor to understand more readily the reactions and attitudes of his employees. He should, however, evaluate any theories and conclusions about human motivation both in terms of the setting in which the research was conducted and in terms of his own experience. There are very few absolutes in supervision. Decisions and actions must always be adapted to a particular environment and to the circumstances at hand.

I hope this work will stimulate the reader to see the supervisory job as the exciting, rewarding challenge it truly is.

Since the major part of the book is based on my own experience and observations, I am grateful to the many persons who over the years have shared these experiences with me and who have contributed to my own understanding. Special thanks are due the editors of the American Management Association for their support and encouragement, as well as for their expert professional advice.

MAXINE H. BISHOP

Contents

I

What Is Supervision?

SUPERVISION IS THE ART OF ACCOMPLISHING work through the efforts and abilities of other people. An organization may have several different levels of supervision, some dealing directly with employees doing the work, while others are responsible for subordinate supervisors who oversee the work. Regardless of level, supervision is a *function* consisting of distinctive duties and responsibilities and employing a unique set of principles, practices, and skills.

Difference Between Working and Supervising

A useful way to define supervising is to distinguish it from working. In *working,* the employee has physical contact with the work itself. This is true no matter what the work is. It may be assembling a part in a manufacturing plant. It may be purchasing materials or supplies or auditing a set of books. It may be designing a bridge. It may be planning and conducting a sophisticated research project. It may be giving nursing care to a sick patient, or planning special diets, or performing laboratory tests. It may be selling—either to retail customers or to business establishments. It may be answering telephone inquiries, or typing correspondence, or filing.

No matter how diverse the tasks may be, they all have one thing in common. In every case, the employee has physical *contact* with the work (at least with his portion of it). He has a great deal of control over it. Unless he is on a timed production line, he can control whether he gets started immediately or whether he first wastes half an hour chatting with a fellow employee or daydreaming. He can control whether he works quickly or slowly, whether he turns out a high-quality product or a sloppy one, whether he applies himself steadily every day or whether he is frequently absent. Finally, he can control whether he plunges into the work, really giving it his best in thought and energy, or whether he does his assignment half-heartedly, using only a small part of his brain for his job and reserving the rest to think about his family, his social life, a hobby, or a private business deal.

The supervisor, on the other hand, does not have physical contact with the work. The employee comes *between* the supervisor and the work to be done. This means that the supervisor has only remote control. Whether the work is done, or how well it is done, or whether it is done on time depends upon the extent to which he can control the employee actually *doing* the work. Yet it is the super-

visor who is fully responsible and accountable for seeing
that the work is done. For example, if the assembly workers produce at too low a level, if the designer comes up
with a defective bridge, if the research project never gets
off the ground, or if sales people fail to sell—in short, if
the work is not done properly and on time—it is the
supervisor who is blamed. If the work failure occurs frequently and is not corrected, his job is in jeopardy just
as surely as is the job of the offending employee.

The supervisor, in other words, is *accountable* for the
work turned out by others. Accountability is what really
distinguishes the supervisor's job. If this essential ingredient is missing, the job is not supervisory. For example,
a person may train new employees, answer their technical
questions, or inspect their work, but he is not a supervisor
unless *he* and not someone else is clearly accountable for
the employees' work.

Accountability, moreover, must extend over the whole
gamut of an employee's job performance—not just the
accomplishment of a given task. It must include the employee's attendance and punctuality, his relations with the
public and his co-workers, his training, the adequacy of his
knowledge and skill, and his conduct on the job.

Union contracts frequently use the phrase "authority
to hire and fire" to determine whether a position is supervisory. This phrase epitomizes accountability. First-line
supervisors in government or in large organizations frequently do not have *final* authority to hire and fire. They
must, however, have the authority to "effectively recommend" these actions if they are to qualify as supervisors.

This definition of a supervisor excludes a host of employees who probably consider themselves supervisors—
such as leadmen or team leaders or senior employees who

answer technical questions. These individuals perform a vital service in an organization, and they are acquiring experience that will be valuable in preparing them to be supervisors. But they are not now supervisors because they are not accountable for the whole range of an employee's performance.

Difference Between Supervisors and Managers

Supervisors are not the same as managers. True, in most cases managers have supervisory duties, but they also have additional, broader functions that set them apart. Managers usually are responsible for determining the overall objectives of an organization, for initiating long-range planning and forecasting, for establishing policies, for developing the organizational structure, and for setting up financial planning and control. They also coordinate disparate activities. For example, a manager in a manufacturing company must coordinate purchasing, manufacturing, and sales. A manager frequently must represent his organization to outside groups such as unions, government agencies, and community organizations. Supervisors normally do not have these broad responsibilities. Moreover, the manager usually has a fair amount of authority to determine *what* work is to be done, while the supervisor is most often responsible for accomplishing a preassigned mission, although he usually has considerable leeway in deciding *how* to accomplish it.

This book is not concerned with the broader duties of the manager, but it *is* addressed to the supervisory part of his job—his dealings with subordinates in getting work done. The skills he needs for this phase of his job are the same skills required of supervisors.

Role of Technical Competence

What skills must one have to perform the supervisory function? First of all, technical competence in the work being supervised is a must. Without it a person cannot be an effective supervisor, no matter how capable he may be in other ways. A supervisor must understand the work and be able to evaluate its difficulty and judge how long an employee should take to complete it. Supervisors who are technically deficient usually present a sorry spectacle as they try to bluff their way through. Employees seem to have an uncanny ability to size up supervisors, and they are quick to spot one who is technically incompetent. They will not respect or follow him. They may amiably tolerate him and humor him, so that he thinks he has a fine relationship with them. Nevertheless, they have learned to manipulate him, and in no time at all they (not he) are running the show. A supervisor who does not have strong technical knowledge of the work is usually painfully aware of his shortcomings. His resulting lack of self-confidence and assertiveness will nearly always prevent him from applying other skills to his job, even if he has them.

If we look at the broad spectrum of supervisors in business, industry, government, and nonprofit organizations, we may conclude that the major weakness in supervisors is *not* lack of technical competence. Many supervisors who come up from the ranks are promoted largely *because of* their knowledge of the work and probably because they perform it better than other employees do. If they are deficient as supervisors, it is most likely to be because they lack those other skills that are an integral part of supervision—skills that are the subject of this book.

The subject of technical competence should not be

treated lightly, however. Individuals who are promoted from the ranks do not always have expert knowledge of the work. Maybe their bosses merely *think* they do, or their bosses may think they have other skills, such as the ability to get along with people. The virtues of loyalty, dependability, and industriousness play a significant role in promotions. These qualities, though essential to an organization, have nothing to do with technical competence or with supervisory success.

Organizational Climate and Technical Competence

Organizations are fascinating entities. They are not orderly, rational beings, as they are commonly assumed to be. In fact, they may be quite irrational and their behavior quite aberrant. The personalities and abilities of those individuals with power—the managers—create the climate of the organization, which can be of overwhelming importance in determining the kinds of people hired and the kinds of people promoted to supervisory positions. If the managers in an organization are not technically competent themselves, they will select and promote individuals who are *less* competent than they. In other words, technical incompetence at the managerial level begets technical incompetence all down the line.

One of the heroes of management folklore is the manager who is not very good himself but surrounds himself with good men. This is indeed a mythical person. For a technically incompetent manager to surround himself with subordinates who are experts would be utterly contrary to human nature and would require a magnanimity and lack of ego that are hard to imagine. The manager who lacks technical competence is most likely to surround himself with subordinates who (he thinks) will not recognize his inadequacies.

The manager of one large unit had a grade-school education. He had been with the organization for many years and had come up through the ranks to his present high level. His promotions had been based not so much on technical competence as on loyalty, long service, industriousness, dependability, and respect for his superiors. Although the unit had grown considerably in size and did work that was quasi-professional, it did not contain a single college graduate. Individuals were hired with virtually no background in the work and then were trained on the job in the day-to-day operations. Those promoted to supervisory positions invariably were people who had been in the unit for many years, who worked hard but never questioned any aspect of the work or the methods used, who were intensely loyal and deferential to the manager, and who showed admiration and respect for him. As a result of this policy the entire unit became stagnant—clinging to antiquated work methods, performing needless detail, and resisting all efforts by top management to streamline operations. The unit was incapable of rising to new demands placed upon it for analytical and creative endeavor.

Deliberate De-emphasis of Technical Competence

There seems to be a tendency in some quarters to downgrade the need for technical competence and to concentrate on other skills. One often hears it said that a good manager can manage anything. Two factors seem to be largely responsible for this point of view. Organizations may have had bad experiences with supervisors who were technically capable but administratively ineffective. They might then try to solve a problem by concentrating on presumed managerial skills rather than on technical ability.

The second factor is technological change, which has had a tremendous impact on the nature of work and has produced a constant demand for new skills and retraining. What is technical competence today may be obsolete skill tomorrow. It is even being said that in years to come the average person may be expected to change careers several times because of job obsolescence. Some believe the remedy for this situation is to de-emphasize technical skill and try to produce supervisors and managers who are "generalists" and who are adaptable and flexible and can move freely from one kind of work to another.

This notion has considerable validity when applied to *managerial* rather than supervisory jobs, and it illustrates vividly an essential difference between managers and supervisors. It may be true that a good manager can manage anything at the top levels; witness the ease with which top executives can move between entirely unrelated industries or between industry and government. One should remember, however, that managers do not acquire their competence overnight. Through a long succession of experiences—coupled, frequently, with study—they have acquired understanding of how organizations function, knowledge of the various processes of governing an enterprise, and know-how in dealing effectively with people.

A good manager also is almost invariably an expert in some field, such as finance, sales, engineering, or manufacturing. When a company goes outside its own field to employ a top executive, it usually does so because he has particular strengths or talents that the company badly needs.

Finally, the good manager has certain skills that set him apart, not only from supervisors, but also from mediocre or poor managers. Foremost is the ability to select subordinates who are highly trained in their particular fields, to use the skills and knowledge of these subordinates in the most effective way, and to mold them into an integrated, productive team. Equally important, the good manager has a broad perspective of methods and procedures. If basic segments of the work can be eliminated or radically transformed by technology, he knows how to take advantage of these changes and how to adjust the organization to accommodate them.

The average supervisor cannot possibly have these broad skills and this knowledge. He has not had the variety and breadth of experience needed to acquire them. To make him the overseer of work that he does not understand is like throwing a person who cannot swim into deep water. It is true that a supervisor should be flexible and adaptable so that he may be retrained in some other work if his technical competence becomes obsolete through technological change. He must be *retrained,* however, before he can supervise the new work. The following example is a case in point.

The case of Mr. Wilson. The accounts receivable section of a firm was having many problems. The supervisor knew credit and collections work thoroughly, but he could not get along with the employees, all of whom were women. He was tactless in dealing with them and made sudden and frequent changes in work assignments without any discussion with them. Turnover was high. None of the girls really knew what she was supposed to do because jobs were always being changed. The amount of money outstanding in accounts receivable was steadily increasing, as was the number of bad debts written off. The firm manager finally induced the supervisor to resign, after which he started looking for a replacement.

He made a deliberate decision to de-emphasize technical competence. After interviewing many candidates, he selected Mr. Wilson, a personable young man who had had no credit and collections experience but had supervised a fair-size group of statistical clerks in an insurance agency. His job had been abolished when the statistical work was automated. Mr. Wilson made a good appearance, which was desirable in dealing with customers. He had a friendly, open personality, which would enable him to get along with the girls. The manager told him about some of the problems with his predecessor and cautioned him against making a lot of changes lest he upset the employees.

Things seemed to go well for about two months. Turnover began to decrease, and the girls apparently liked their new supervisor. The manager began to relax. When he received the bimonthly report on the status of accounts, however, he had a rude shock. Receivables had shot up alarmingly. At about the same time, he began to receive telephone calls and letters from irate customers complaining about mix-ups and mistakes in their bills or about rude treatment over the telephone.

The manager talked repeatedly to Mr. Wilson about these serious problems. He could offer no explanation for them except to say that he was doing his best, but he had inherited a mess which would take some time to straighten out. He added that he did not want to push the girls too hard because morale was improving and he did not want to jeopardize it.

One day, one of the few remaining older employees in the accounts receivable section asked to see the manager and spilled out a story of utter chaos in the section.

All employees were confused about what they were supposed to do. The work was not getting done; billing was far behind; and inexperienced clerks were answering telephone inquiries from customers and were frequently rude and gave out wrong information. The employee who handled new accounts was making bad mistakes, but Mr. Wilson did not say anything to her because he thought she was good. Discipline had broken down completely. Some of the girls were sitting around doing nothing or going out for coffee and staying an hour or so. According to the employee, Mr. Wilson seemed to be afraid of the girls. He never gave them any assignments or instructions about the work. In fact, he had stopped coming into the main office altogether and just sat in his own office.

The manager, of course, had to evaluate the information given him by the employee. After talking to several of the other older girls as well as to Mr. Wilson, he concluded that the situation in the office was just about as it had been described.

Mr. Wilson's behavior—his withdrawal from the office situation—is rather typical of a person without technical competence in the work he is supervising. A good *manager* might have overcome his lack of technical knowledge by enlisting the ideas and cooperation of the girls in getting the office organized and duties assigned. Mr. Wilson, however, did not begin to have the managerial experience, self-confidence, determination, toughness, and ability to size up people's skills that such an achievement would have required. He was himself a victim of technological change, having been displaced from his old job because of automation. He probably could have adapted to a new career if he had been *retrained* in credit and collections. Moreover, had he been placed in charge of an office that was stable instead of in crisis, he would have had a period of grace in which to learn the work and to develop self-confidence before being called upon to make major supervisory decisions.

The policy of de-emphasizing technical competence might have worked if Mr. Wilson had come equipped with real managerial skills. However, he was not and there is no indication that the manager of the firm really knew what skills he was seeking. A nice appearance and a good personality are a far cry from managerial competence. In any case, it is extremely risky to expect a first-line supervisor to have real managerial know-how. He will not have had the kind of experience that would have provided it.

Placing administrators over professional work. A somewhat different situation is the tendency to place administrators over professional work—that is, specialized work requiring education equivalent to four years or more of college. The rationale for this decision is similar to the one just described—de-emphasizing technical competence in favor of other skills. Many organizations have experienced difficulties with the quality of supervision and direction given by professional employees and, consequently, have attempted to separate the professional work itself from the supervision and administration of it.

This solution to the problem may be a success or it may be a disaster. The secret lies in a thorough understanding of the nature of the work and in making a clear distinction between *administration* and *line supervision* of the professional work. Hospitals offer examples of both the success and the failure of this approach.

Twenty-five years ago, most hospitals were headed by physicians. Some smaller ones were directed by registered nurses. Today, it is rare to find either physicians or nurses administering hospitals. They have been successfully supplanted by professional administrators. In this case, the manifold administrative and managerial problems of the modern hospital (financial management, labor relations, community relations, organizational planning and coordination) could be successfully spun off from direct patient care, which was left in the hands of the physicians and nurses. In fact, the growth of hospitals and the rapid expansion of hospital and medical care made this separation imperative.

The dietary services within hospitals have also afforded the same successful separation of professional patient care and managerial functions. Twenty years ago, virtually every hospital dietary service was headed by a chief dietitian. This plan of organization is now rapidly disappearing. An increasing number of hospitals today have commercially trained food-service managers in charge of food procurement, cooking, and service to the patients. In fact, many hospitals now have contracts with institutional food caterers to provide all these services. Dietitians are solely responsible for planning menus and therapeutic diets and for patient education and consultation.

The nature of the work of a hospital dietary department has made this separation of responsibilities a natural. Dietitians were never trained to run a commercial food service any more than doctors and nurses were trained in financial management, labor relations, and other phases of hospital administration. The important point to emphasize is this: Not only did the nature of the work make possible a clean separation between professional and managerial functions, but a clear distinction also was made between administration and line supervision of the professional work. The hospital administrator does not attempt to supervise the physician or the nurse caring for a patient. Neither does the commercial food-service manager attempt to supervise the dietitian in the preparation of therapeutic diets or in other professional aspects of her work.

Many professional organizations—for example, an engineering company, a law firm, or a scientific research unit—may use administrators effectively to handle such purely administrative functions as coordinating cost estimates, budgeting, accounting, contract administration, and personnel relations. If these administrators attempt direct supervision of the professional staff, however, there is almost certain to be trouble.

When hospitals have tried to make administrators the first-line supervisors of professional workers, they have failed. Such was the case with a large metropolitan hospital that had chronic problems with its clinical laboratory. Payroll costs were excessive. The laboratory was overstaffed, yet overtime was high. Reports of test results were late in being returned to the wards that requested them, and doctors were complaining. What better solution, the administrator thought, than to put a *manager* (rather than a physician or a technician) in charge. Possibly he could control the payroll costs and resolve the other problems.

An individual with many years of administrative experience was made laboratory supervisor. Since he knew nothing about laboratory work, he was loath to evaluate the technicians, their performance, or their workloads. Without such an evaluation, it was impossible to get to the heart of the problem, let alone correct it. The only thing left for the administrative supervisor to concern himself with were largely clerical tasks, such as ordering supplies and equipment and keeping time cards and personnel records. So the problems remained.

Hospitals have had similar results when they have tried to improve supervision on nursing units by introducing administrative ward managers. Since they cannot supervise the employees in direct patient care, the ward managers have become glorified clerks. In this case and in the laboratory case just cited, there are not enough high-level administrative duties to split off from the professional work. Thus one result of attempting to make administrative persons first-line supervisors of professional workers is for the administrative supervisors to become an excess overhead cost.

There can be other results. A specialized government agency was dissatisfied with the quality of supervision given by its professional staff. As a solution, it introduced administrative officers into each of its major divisions. According to the plan for separation of responsibilities, the various professional supervisors were to direct the technical aspects of the work, while the administrative officers were to handle all administrative and personnel matters. The administrative officers interpreted this ambiguous assignment of responsibility as placing them *between* the professional supervisors and their employees and *between* the staff offices of the agency (such as personnel and finance) and all the line officers of their respective divisions.

Over the years this arrangement fashioned an entirely new organizational structure for the agency. The staff officers became advisers to the different administrative officers, who established their own personnel policies, developed independent budgets for their divisions, and set up separate units to handle supplies and mail, messenger, and duplicating services. In effect, each division became an independent entity, pursuing its own goals and policies without regard for the rest of the agency.

The professional supervisors willingly abdicated their responsibility for the employees assigned to them. The administrative officers selected new employees and assigned them to various professional supervisors. If a supervisor was not satisfied with an employee's work, he said nothing to the employee. Instead, he told the administrative officer, who then attempted to correct the situation by talking to the employee, by reassigning him to another supervisor, or by asking the agency's personnel office to reassign the person to another division. The administrative officers, rather than the supervisors, prepared all periodic performance reports on employees. They wrote job descriptions, and they developed and administered their own promotion plans.

This situation resulted in nearly insurmountable problems of communication and coordination. There was duplication of effort among the different divisions and between the divisions and the staff offices. It was almost impossible for the agency head to introduce new policies, to modify the agency's objectives, or to give it new ones. The professional employees were underused and underdeveloped, and they were confused about their duties and the goals of the agency. Morale was hurt by inconsistency of promotion policies among divisions. Promotions were slow in one division and very rapid in another, and there was no movement of personnel across division lines.

In this case, a separation *was* made between the professional aspects of the work and those that were considered to be administrative, but it was an undesirable separation which did great harm to the agency. Essential supervisory functions such as staff training and development, discussing employees' work with them, preparing performance reports, interviewing and selecting employees, and recommending promotions were separated out as administrative duties. These are responsibilities that no one but the line supervisor should assume. Instead of improving supervision, this arrangement just about destroyed it.

This discussion of the importance of technical competence can be summarized with these observations: Technical competence is most essential at the first line of supervision, and there can be no substitute for it at that level. It becomes less important, and managerial skills become more important, at the higher echelons of management. Administrative personnel cannot successfully be made first-line supervisors of technical or professional workers. They can, however, be used to advantage when a clearcut separation can be made between the professional and the administrative aspects of the work—provided that such a separation is truly desirable.

Conceptual and Interpersonal Skills

Having said this about technical competence, we may proceed with the business of this book, which is about those other skills and abilities that are requisite to effective supervision. These skills and abilities fall into two broad categories, conceptual and interpersonal.

A supervisor must be able to *conceive* the work he supervises, both in its wholeness and in its multiplicity. He must mentally identify all the fragments and particles that make up the work, and he must see them in various combinations and arrangements until they form an integrated whole.

Supervised work is like a mass of dough. A talented baker can knead and work the dough, separate it, recombine it, and separate it again into pastries of all sizes and shapes, each of which is an artistic triumph. An unimaginative baker sees a mass of dough as just that—a mass of dough to be put into the oven. The result of his labor is something to be eaten without relish or appreciation.

Too many supervisors view the work they supervise as something static and unchangeable. They see the tasks and jobs of subordinates as predetermined. These supervisors produce work like the bread of the unimaginative baker—something that is eaten without relish. It may never occur to them that the elements of the work could be rearranged and reshaped in ways that would produce finished work that more nearly resembled an artistic triumph.

Rarely does a supervisor lack authority to make changes and improvements in the planning and organization of the work under him. A creative supervisor will experiment with ways of organizing and reorganizing the flow of work, ways of assigning duties to make the best use of employees' abilities, ways of motivating and stimulating employees by giving them more challenge and responsibility.

It is of course impractical for a supervisor to make *real* changes in the work flow and assignments all the time. If he did, he would soon have chaos as the work piled up. He would also be faced with a rebellion by employees who disliked having their jobs changed every other day. He must therefore carry out his experiments in his own laboratory; that is, in his mind. He must mentally plan and organize the work in a variety of ways. He must ask himself such questions as these: Where are bottlenecks that can be eliminated? What procedures and tasks have become obsolete and should be discontinued? How can duties be regrouped to make best use of the more experienced and capable employees? Where should supervisory controls be placed to make sure the work is done? How much volume should be assigned to each employee? What tasks should the supervisor do himself? What plans and schedules could be used to insure that essential steps are completed on time and in the proper sequence or that supplies and equipment are on hand when needed? These and other questions are part of the mental process that a supervisor must go through. The skills that he applies to the process are *conceptual* skills.

Just as conceptual skills are intellectual, *interpersonal* skills are social and emotional. The interpersonal part of supervision is commonly referred to as "human relations," although this term has lost much of its meaning through overuse and misuse. Interpersonal skills embrace the innumerable ways a supervisor talks and acts in direct personal contact with employees. Do the supervisor's words and actions come across to the employee the way the supervisor wants them to? Do his words and actions inspire the employee to follow the supervisor and to do the best job he can? Do the supervisor's words and actions result in an increase in the knowledge and skill of the employee? Do they give the employee freedom to do a creative job, yet establish proper boundaries of performance? The answers to these questions will, in large measure, reveal the interpersonal skills of the supervisor. Those abstract, imprecise, and largely intuitive qualities of leadership, motivation, and communication are the essence of interpersonal skills.

Supervision, then, can be viewed as two sides of a coin, with conceptual skills on one side and interpersonal skills on the other. These skills complement each other. They are mutually dependent. Unfortunately, they are entirely different kinds of skills. One could be considered introvert, the other extrovert. Many people have one or the other of these skills, but not *both*. Yet to be effective a supervisor must have both.

Some supervisors can visualize the work and think through its multiple aspects; but they lack the emotional calm, maturity, empathy, sensitivity, or insight to deal effectively with human response, human problems, human conflict. Other supervisors have a natural talent for interpersonal relations, but they lack the imagination, acuity, patience, or tenacity to apply real brainpower to planning, organizing, and other conceptual tasks. It is for this reason that we say supervision is truly an art.

2

Organizing for Results

O NE OF THE MOST IMPORTANT CONCEPTUAL skills of a supervisor is the ability to organize the work. He must be able to conceive the work he supervises. And he must be able to visualize it broken down into its component parts and then assembled in many different ways until the most effective combination is found.

The word "organization" is often used indiscriminately to describe many things. It is commonly thought of as a set of charts containing a number of boxes showing various executives and major departments, with connecting lines depicting who reports to whom. This is a superficial and entirely erroneous view of the purpose and nature of organization. Although the building of sound departments at the executive level is vital, there is an equally pressing need (often overlooked) for good organization at the levels where the work is actually performed.

Sometimes the word is confused with systems and procedures. An office may be criticized for not being "organized," whereas what is really meant is that the paperwork procedures used are cumbersome and inefficient. The word also may be confused with the process of planning and scheduling, which will be discussed in a later chapter.

Organization is simply the way in which resources—personnel, equipment, and money—are used. Good organization is a way of using them effectively to obtain the best results in terms of the goals of the enterprise. Poor organization is a way of using these resourses wastefully, producing either poor results or acceptable results at too high a cost.

The process of organization has two major phases: breaking the work down into segments (jobs), each of which can be handled by a single person; and devising a means of coordinating the work of all the different individuals.

There are two major schools of thought regarding organization. At one extreme are the *classical theories,* which are the oldest and also the most generally accepted. They trace their ancestry to the "scientific management" movement of the early part of this century, led by such giants as Frederick Winslow Taylor, Frank and Lillian Gilbreth, and Henry L. Gantt.[1] These pioneers conducted their research entirely in factories, and they were dedicated to the principle of functional specialization.

At the opposite extreme are the *behavioral science theories,* articulated by a number of modern researchers,

[1] See Frederick Winslow Taylor, *Scientific Management,* Harper & Row, Publishers, Inc., New York, 1947; William R. Spriegel and Clark E. Myers (editors), *The Writings of the Gilbreths,* Richard D. Irwin, Inc., Homewood, Ill., 1953; and Henry L. Gantt, *Work, Wages, and Profits,* 2d edition, The Engineering Magazine Co., New York, 1913.

including Chester I. Barnard, Herbert A. Simon, Bernard Bass, E. Wight Bakke, Chris Argyris, and Warren Bennis.[2] A supervisor should understand these opposing theories and evaluate them in the light of his own experience and his own work situation.

Segmenting the Work into Jobs

The way work is broken down into jobs is of primary importance. It determines the kind of people to be employed, how much they will be paid, how long it will take to train them, and frequently what kind of controls should be established over the work. It may also have a less obvious but equally powerful effect on morale, employee development, and employee relations.

According to the classical theories, jobs should be confined as far as possible to a single function. They should not contain duties that are too complex or are unrelated. And there should be no overlapping or duplication of functions among different positions. Furthermore, authority should be commensurate with responsibilty, and duties and responsibilities should be set forth in writing and should be clearly understood by the incumbents of the jobs.

The behavioral scientists challenge these views. They

[2] See Chester I. Barnard, *The Functions of the Executive,* Harvard University Press, Cambridge, Mass., 1938; Herbert A. Simon, *Administrative Behavior,* 2d edition, The Macmillan Company, New York, 1947; Bernard Bass, *Organizational Psychology,* Allyn & Bacon, Inc., Boston, Mass., 1965; E. Wight Bakke, *The Fusion Process,* Labor and Management Center, Yale University, New Haven, Conn., 1953; Chris Argyris, *Personality and Organization,* Harper & Row, Publishers, Inc., New York, 1957; and Warren Bennis, *Changing Organizations,* McGraw-Hill Book Company, New York, 1966.

hold that the classical theories fail to consider human personality or motivation. They believe that, instead of being restricted to single functions, jobs should have a wide assortment of tasks to make them more challenging and interesting and to afford more growth and development for employees (and, consequently, for the organization). They emphasize the need for job enrichment, and many researchers think that even the most routine jobs can be enlarged by permitting the incumbents to make some decisions about how the work is done.

The classical idea that authority should be commensurate with responsibility is viewed as unrealistic and self-defeating by the behavioral scientists. Authority, they believe, is an intangible that accrues to a person because of his value, his technical competence and knowledge, and the esteem in which he is held by others. It cannot be handed down from above. The attempt to assign authority fosters irresponsibility for organizational objectives and buck-passing, since employees can always plead that they did all they could and had no authority to do more. The solution, in the eyes of the behavioral scientists, is for organizations to stress group consensus and wide participation in decision making.

Just as they believe that overspecialization can stymie employee growth, these experts maintain that overdefinition of duties can serve as a straitjacket and a psychological barrier to maximum performance. It is their view that formal job descriptions open up the possibility of jurisdictional disputes, concentration on limits of responsibility rather than on objectives, and evasion of work. They decry the establishment of rigid boundaries for jobs. Let them be fluid enough, they say, to spill over into other areas of work.

Work Coordination

Coordinating the work of different individuals is a difficult and complex phase of organization and certainly a critical one. No matter how the work is segmented into jobs, an enterprise cannot function unless an effective means is devised for meshing together all the various activities.

The classical theories of organization enunciate two major principles in this area: unity of command and span of control. *Unity of command* means that someone should be responsible for supervising all essential activities and that each person should be accountable to only a single supervisor. It is essential that every employee know whom he reports to and who reports to him. Moreover, the chain of command should be recognized and followed at all times.

Span of control refers to the number of subordinates who should logically report to a single supervisor. The classical theorists believe there is an optimum number of subordinates that a supervisor can direct effectively. The number should not be so great that the supervisor is unable to give adequate attention to each one. Nor should it be so small that the supervisor either has too little to do himself or is inclined to oversupervise his employees. There is disagreement as to what the optimum number is. Some classical theorists say an executive should have no more than three subordinates reporting to him; others say six. Still others say five to seven subordinates is optimum at the executive level, while up to twenty-four is acceptable for first-line supervisors.

The unity of command concept is severely dealt with by the behavioral scientists. They say it forces an organization into a mechanical mold in which a formally appointed leader frequently knows less than those he leads about the work or the problems facing the group. They urge greater permissiveness and greater sharing of leadership among all members of a group so that each person will feel free to suggest new approaches and those with the most ability to solve particular problems can assume the proper leadership roles.

The idea that the chain of command must be followed at all times receives an even harsher indictment. According to the behavioral scientists, this rule creates tremendous problems of communication if it is strictly enforced. A subordinate three levels down in one organization cannot communicate a suggestion or information or a request directly to his counterpart in another organization. His communication must go up through his chain of command and down through his counterpart's chain before contact can be made. Bypassing some levels in the chain often creates resentment and hurt feelings on the part of those bypassed. Each level through which a communication must pass serves as a potential bottleneck. It may stop the communication or distort it and pass it along in greatly altered form.

Similarly, the behavioral scientists criticize the classical rules regarding span of control because they create a steep, vertical hierarchy with excessive layers of supervision. This structure requires elaborate reporting systems and blocks the flow of communication. Moreover, it creates a rigid, unwieldy organization that cannot respond quickly and adequately to changes in environment. It also creates morale problems by forming a caste system among the various echelons, with employees at the lower levels believing that they are second- or third-class citizens.

To replace these classical concepts, the behavioral scientists advocate much less structure and less formality, with the emphasis on goals and objectives. They see organizational groupings centered around tasks. The goals of the task should be established first, they say; then employee groups should be organized around the task. The groups should be temporary. When the task is completed or changed, the membership of the group should change. Members of the group would then be deeply committed to the goals of the task. They would communicate freely with one another and would involve themselves completely in solving problems that interfere with the attainment of objectives. Each group member would have an opportunity to assume responsibility for task achievement, with material rewards going to those who accept and hold responsibility and who overcome job challenges.

Pros and Cons of the Two Theories

As was mentioned earlier, the classical theories owe much to the scientific management movement, whose milieu was the manufacturing plant. The classical ideas regarding the segmenting of work into jobs are a corollary to the techniques of mass production. The factory assembly line is notable for its precise and orderly separation of functions, for the smooth flow of work from one operation to the next, and for the tight control and coordination that keep the system running efficiently. It is essential in this kind of operation to break down jobs into their simplest elements so that methods and motions can be studied and standardized, jobs can be timed, the amount of training can be held to a minimum, and several different elements of the work can be performed simultaneously by different employees.

Moreover, it is imperative that duties be prescribed rather rigidly, spelled out in detail, and understood perfectly by the employees. There is no place in the assembly-line system for the overlapping of functions or the spilling over of duties from one job to another. This manner of organizing the work permits close control over operations, but at the same time it creates serious employee morale problems stemming from boredom, alienation from the company, and dissatisfaction with working conditions.

The same single-function concept carried over into other activities of the manufacturing firm and was responsible for the functional separation of sales, advertising, personnel management, accounting, purchasing, engineering, research and development, and so forth. The concept creates problems of the kind that are decried by the behavioral scientists when it is applied too rigidly to the organization of work *within* many of these ancillary departments. Research and development, sales, advertising, engineering, and general management all demand imagination and creativity, and jobs should be structured in a way that will provide the most nourishment for these qualities. They usually thrive best in a loosely structured job context rather than in a clearly defined one.

The factory assembly line is no longer predominant as an employer of labor. Many assembly-line operations have been automated, and manufacturing has itself been surpassed as the major provider of jobs by the fast-growing service industries, nonprofit organizations, and government. Not only has the job mix changed; workers have changed also. Today's employees are better educated, more restless, and more easily bored than their counterparts of 20 years ago. They have higher aspirations and a higher regard for their own potential. The classical theories of job organization simply cannot be applied en masse today, and the behavioral scientists have rendered a valuable service by pointing out their defects.

Yet the supervisor would be ill-advised to swing completely over to the behaviorist concept of job organization. Fluid, unstructured jobs that spill over into one another can become a confused tangle, with employees not knowing what they are supposed to do and the work not being done. To administer this kind of job structure requires a very high degree of supervisory skill. Overstaffing and overpermissiveness all too often result from the lack of enough form and structure to the work. The truth is that both the classical and the behaviorist concepts have their place, and it is the function of the supervisor to know under what circumstances each is most valid. In many cases, a synthesis of the two points of view can result in the most dynamic organization.

When Jobs Require Structure

Manual jobs that employ relatively unskilled workers usually function best when they are structured along classical lines, which is to say when they are confined to a single function, specified in detail, and clearly understood by the incumbents. The job of hotel chambermaid is an example. The most efficient way of organizing this job is to assign a particular number of rooms to be cleaned and provide the maid with a written description stating exactly what is to be done in the cleaning of a room. The job description can be a simple list of tasks. It is a useful training device, it serves as a reminder to the maid, and it also obviates the need for close supervision. A supervisor can easily check the completed rooms against the task list to make sure everything has been done properly.

One hotel tried a more unstructured method of assigning maids in the belief that it would be good for morale and also increase efficiency. The hotel assigned maids to work in teams of two. The teams were assigned to a specific area, but the way they accomplished the work was left to them. It soon developed that the work was not being done. On checking, the supervisor found that, where formerly one maid had changed a bed, now two were doing it and taking nearly as long as one had before. The maids were wasting time deciding what each one was to do, they were duplicating each other's work, and some of the cleaning was being overlooked because each thought the other had done it. They were frustrated by their inability to complete their work.

Food preparation is another example of work that had best be clearly defined and structured. Not only are relatively low-skilled employees used, but there is also an urgency to complete advance food preparation before the mealtime rush begins. These factors militate against a loose, informal assignment of work. Most tasks that have a tight time deadline, whether they are food service or preparation of newspaper copy, should be organized into very distinct jobs, with the duties of each clearly defined and understood.

Emergency situations, or work in which the consequence of error is great, also favor the classical form of organization. A fire-fighting crew does not have time to reach group consensus as to who should do what. Neither can it wait for leadership to emerge from the group. Likewise, each member of an airline maintenance crew must have clearly defined responsibilities because the consequences of oversight or neglect are grave.

When Production Is a Prime Factor

Clerical operations in which production is an essential consideration are often more effective when they are organized on a single-function basis and when duties are prescribed. The billing of patient accounts in a hospital consists of several distinct steps. The patients' insurance coverage is verified with the carrier as soon as possible after the patient is admitted. Immediately after discharge (or at periodic intervals if the hospital stay is lengthy) the insurance carrier is billed for the insured portion and the patient is billed for the balance. Follow-up on payments due from insurance carriers and from patients completes the cycle.

One supervisor organized this work, which involved four clerks, in a way that she thought would make the work most challenging. Each clerk was assigned a segment of the alphabet and made completely responsible for the accounts of all patients whose last names fell within her segment. She verified insurance coverage, billed insurance carriers and patients, and followed up on payments. The follow-up included sending out collection letters or telephoning patients to request payment.

The results were disappointing. The billing was not kept up to date, and there was insufficient follow-up on delinquent accounts. The time of the clerks was dissipated when they switched back and forth from one task to another. Each morning they had a group of new admissions whose insurance had to be verified. It was often late in the day by the time they finished this task, especially if they had one or two complicated insurance cases. They usually did not finish their billing each day and had no time at all for collections follow-up.

The supervisor achieved improved results when she

restructured the work along purely functional lines. One clerk was assigned full time to verify all insurance. It was found that she could save time by consolidating all calls to the same carrier and by sending out written requests to the largest carrier, whereas previously the clerks had used the telephone to verify most of the insurance. Two clerks were assigned to billing and follow-up until payment was received from the insurance carrier. The fourth clerk was assigned to follow up on all uninsured balances due from patients, including the collection of delinquent accounts.

Once the clerks could devote full time to the particular task at hand, they were able to produce a great deal more and to keep the work current. The new plan also revealed that the clerks had aptitudes for some tasks and not for others. One who had been very slow in billing was found to have a special flair for dealing with patients on unpaid accounts. Another clerk whose patient relationships had been poor proved to be an excellent biller.

As we have seen, several kinds of work situations are best organized along the classical lines of single functions, carefully prescribed duties, and clearly defined responsibilities. These are manual work that employs relatively unskilled workers, tasks that involve time deadlines or emergencies or in which the consequence of error or oversight is serious, and work in which production is of prime importance. In organizing these jobs, however, there are several cautions that the supervisor should heed.

1. Do not overspecialize the work to the point that the employee becomes a mechanical robot. Give the job as much integrity as possible so that the employee may have the satisfaction of seeing a finished job. The hotel maid, for example, is assigned a specific number of rooms and

a specific set of duties, but she is responsible for *entire* rooms. It would be a mistake to break up the work so that one maid changes all the beds, another maid cleans all the bathrooms, and yet another does all the dusting and vacuuming. A functional arrangement of this kind would deny the employee the pride that she could derive from seeing a completely clean room, and it would introduce a deadly monotony into the job.

2. Do not rigidly structure jobs and then expect employees to be willing to stay in them indefinitely. Everyone likes change now and then. Give them a chance to learn other jobs whenever possible in order to develop their skills and increase their interest. Having them fill in for individuals who are on vacation is one way to give them more experience. Frequent rotation from job to job, however, is undesirable. Most employees want stability in their work. They like to know specifically what they will be doing when they come to work in the morning, and they want a job of their own, with which they can identify and for which they can be responsible.

3. Be alert to detect employees with the interest and ability to do more advanced work. The structure of jobs should not make them a prison. If an employee seems to be straining against the barriers of his job, give him something more difficult to do or something new to learn. Perhaps having him help train new employees would be a challenge to him.

4. Be sure that you have not specialized any job so much that it lacks enough volume to keep the employee completely busy. Many employees are bored to death with their jobs simply because they do not have enough to do. In the hospital billing case cited earlier, it would have been ill-advised to set up a separate job for insurance

verification unless there had been enough work to keep a full-time employee busy. Jobs that have too little volume are not only boring; they are extremely costly as well.

Professional and Managerial Jobs

The behavioral science theories have a good deal of validity when applied to professional and managerial areas of work. If initiative, imagination, and creativity are the principal requirements of jobs, a rigid, single-function, closely prescribed structure can be devastating.

Small organizations rarely have problems of too much structure. If the research and development unit of a company consists of one engineer, there can be no problem of structure. The engineer probably has wide latitude and flexibility in setting his objectives, planning his time, and applying his efforts. He usually can pursue many avenues of investigation so long as he eventually produces a marketable product. Suppose, however, that the company grows, decides to expand its research and development unit, and appoints the engineer as its supervisor. How does he divide up the work for best results?

Assume that the engineer–supervisor has decided that the company's research program will require four top-grade professionals: a chemist, a physicist, a chemical engineer, and a mechanical engineer. He then decides to employ three support people for each of these top-grade men (twelve support employees in all). One will be a fully qualified but more junior professional in each of the scientific fields from which the top men were chosen. Two will be subprofessionals who will make drawings and sketches, build prototypes, and test products. Two secretaries will round out the staff.

The supervisor now has eighteen employees under him. He has several alternative ways of organizing the work. He may separate it by the fields of science involved; that is, chemistry, physics, chemical engineering, and mechanical engineering. He may establish a separate branch for each of these specialties, to include the top scientist as chief and three assistants (one fully qualified junior professional and two subprofessionals). He may organize the work by stage of research; that is, basic research, applied research, product development, and testing. Or he may organize the work by product class, establishing separate branches for each major class. Each branch would in effect have the services of one-half the time of one secretary. In all three plans suggested, the jobs would be structured. There would be very definite job boundaries. The staff of a particular branch would perform work for which that branch was responsible. The division of work among the members of each branch would also be clearly delineated.

We might now speculate on some of the things likely to happen in this research and development unit. We could anticipate that the junior professionals might soon become quite restive as their work constantly bumped up against the assigned responsibilities of another branch or of their own branch chief. The matter of authority could easily become an irritant, particularly if one of the branch chiefs were weak in professional knowledge or capacity, or unimaginative in developing new ideas, and the junior professional under him were the opposite. Every idea of the junior would have to be submitted to the branch chief for approval. If the ideas were frequently rejected or if they just died because of lack of decision by the branch chief, we might expect the assistant soon to lose interest. He might leave the organization, or, if he stayed, he might become passive about the work and do no more than was required. The lack of interest and challenge would soon infect the subprofessionals and even the secretaries.

Moreover, we could expect jurisdictional conflicts among the four branch chiefs as to who had responsibility for a project. Competition among the four would be inevitable. This might be healthy, but it also might be destructive if it degenerated into blame-fixing or buck-passing. Conflicts about the time of the two secretaries would be practically assured. One branch would claim the need for more secretarial help than the others. The issue would probably be resolved only by giving each branch chief a full-time secretary. One branch chief might attempt to build up his branch at the expense of another, or he might scheme to conquer and absorb another branch. Such internecine warfare is common in organizations, and there is little doubt that the rigid structuring of jobs and jurisdictions is a major contributor to it. The research and development supervisor might find that he was spending all his time mediating these squabbles or trying to make decisions when conflicting information was supplied to him.

The job organizations just described fit perfectly the mold of the classical theories, and the consequences that were noted are daily occurrences in large enterprises.

The Unstructured Approach

The supervisor of this unit has another alternative regarding the way he organizes the work. He might decide not to structure it, not to establish branches or other subdivisions, or not to segment and define individual jobs. Instead, he might designate all 18 positions as the research and development group. Jobs would be fluid.

Duties would change with the particular talents of the incumbents and with the needs of the unit. The supervisor would establish objectives for the total unit, and each member of the group (including the subprofessionals) would be expected to produce ideas and suggestions.

The supervisor would have frequent contact with every staff member, both individually and in groups. Ideas generated by individuals would be presented to the whole group. Temporary task forces would be set up to investigate ideas or to pursue particular avenues of research. The task-force leader would be the individual with the most knowledge and skill in the undertaking. More senior employees might be task force members under his direction. His authority over his group would not be handed down from above; it would derive from his professional worth and the respect he commanded of his colleagues. There would be no permanent bosses and subordinates in this structure other than the research and development supervisor. Monetary rewards and recognition would go to those who contribute the most to the department's objectives.

A loose, informal organization of this kind has the potential for producing a stimulating climate for new ideas and a tremendous opportunity for individual growth and development. Success is not guaranteed, however. A great deal depends upon the skill and leadership of the supervisor. Interaction between him and each staff member is essential. The group members must respect him professionally, and they must have confidence in his judgment, fairness, and open-mindedness. He must make accurate appraisals of the abilities and contributions of each member, and he must be able to detect and develop latent talents. He must recognize the fact that many creative people are "lone wolves" who dislike groups and do not perform well in them. He must be able to accommodate and encourage these people.

If the supervisor starts playing favorites and building up certain employees at the expense of others, or if the group loses confidence in his judgment, this method of organization will certainly fail. The group will organize itself into cliques and warring factions.

There are many other kinds of work where a skillful supervisor may experiment with this approach. The principal criterion for its use should be the need to develop creativity, imagination, and initiative. The kind of staff employed is also a major determinant of success or failure. This type of organization will not transform a staff that is dull, listless, and unimaginative; it may, however, shake people out of their lethargy if they have dormant talents that have been encrusted with indifference.

Task Group Versus Unity of Command and Span of Control

The research and development case just described illustrates the differences between the classical and behaviorist views regarding coordination of work. The supervisor could have established separate branches, with clear boundaries of responsibility and authority and with jobs within the branches firmly structured. This type of organization would have satisfied the unity of command and span of control concepts of the classical theories. Someone would have been responsible for all essential activities, and each person would have been accountable to a single supervisor. Each person would have known whom he reported to and who reported to him. Each branch chief would have supervised three subordinates. He could have given adequate attention to each and could comfortably have supervised additional subordinates as the organization grew. Some of the probable conflicts that could result from this type of structure have already been mentioned. There could be still other defects, especially if a rigid chain of command were followed.

Initially, each branch chief would personally supervise the junior professional and the two subprofessionals. However, he might make the junior professional the supervisor of the subprofessionals, thus isolating himself from them. Certainly, if the work expanded to the point where he had two or three junior professionals and an increased number of subprofessionals, he could be expected to establish an intermediate supervisory level. The subprofessionals would then be two layers down and would have no access to the branch chief if the chain of command were faithfully followed. They might have talents and abilities that would never be known to the branch chief. Moreover, they and the junior professionals might never have a chance to develop latent abilities because of the rigid job structure.

In the classical, hierarchical type of organization, it is very easy for potential abilities and talents to go undiscovered and unused. There might be enormous supervisory conflicts between the junior professional and the subprofessionals that would never come to the attention of the branch chief. Neither he nor the subprofessionals would violate the chain of command in order to communicate with one another. Finally, a close, informal working relationship among lower-level staff of different branches would be discouraged by this form of organization.

The supervisor could also have chosen a form of organization that approached the concepts of the behavioral scientists. He could have established an informal, unstructured group without hierarchical levels and without formal job boundaries, placing emphasis on goals and objectives, making each person responsible for producing ideas, and forming temporary task groups for specific undertakings. Leadership of the task groups would have been assumed by those with the most knowledge of the job at hand, regardless of their seniority or pay status.

The conclusion was that the latter form of organization—if handled skillfully by the supervisor—would provide a more favorable climate for new ideas and creativity and would afford individual employees far greater opportunities for growth. This informal structure would be preferred so long as the research and development unit remained fairly small and so long as frequent interaction among *all* members of the unit was desirable. If the unit continued to grow, however, the time would come when the supervisor could not give adequate personal direction to the entire group, and he would have to introduce some intermediate level of supervision. He might then apply a synthesis of the classical and the behaviorist concepts of organization. If he wanted to continue the close working relationships among all members of the group, he might retain the temporary task force form of organization, using his four top men as a coordinating committee to relieve him of some of the direct supervisory responsibility. They could be responsible for reviewing the employee's proposals and recommending for or against new projects. They could follow up on and evaluate the work of the various task groups.

As time went on, the work might justify a functional separation into branches. If so, the number of branches should be held to an absolute minimum, and they should accurately reflect natural divisions in the work rather than arbitarily chosen categories. The supervisor should take care to see that the branch chiefs maintain close relations with each other. He should also insist that they maintain an informal, freely communicating structure rather than erect additional supervisory barriers. Constant emphasis on objectives and results instead of hierarchy or prerogative of position would go far toward maintaining a climate for creativity and growth.

It is often helpful to understand the genesis of concepts and ideas. Just as the classical theories regarding the segmenting of work into jobs owe much to the factory assembly line, so the classical concepts of unity of command and span of control owe much to the oldest organizations in existence—the military and the Roman Catholic Church. Both are pure applications of the classical theories, with precisely defined chains of command and well-formulated spans of control. Both are authoritarian, with orders, policies, and directives formulated at the top and passed down through a vertical hierarchy to the bottom. Their organizational structure was *designed* for transmission from top to bottom; the flow of ideas from bottom to top was not an objective.

Some kinds of endeavor are best organized along classical, authoritarian lines. Police and fire departments are examples. The main objectives of these organizations are not to develop creativity and ideas on the part of the policemen or firemen but to transmit orders and policies formulated at the top, to maintain a tight control over performance, and to develop (through intensive training) reflexes and critical judgment that will enable the policemen and firemen to deal with emergencies.

When the classical form of organization is applied indiscriminately, however, serious problems can result. We hear a great deal about the formal and the informal organization. It is said that the formal organization is not functioning because employees have found a way to bypass it in order to get the work done. When this happens, it means only one thing: that the formal structure is out of tune with the realities and objectives of the enterprise. Although an individual supervisor has little control over the *total* organizational structure, he certainly can control the organization of work under him; and he should know what he is doing when he develops a structure. If he plans to run an authoritarian unit, making all decisions himself and handing directions down to employees, then the classical form of organization is most appropriate. But, if he hopes to encourage participation in decision making or to develop employee initiative and imagination, he should be very cautious about erecting barriers in the form either of overly defined jobs or of subordinate supervisory layers.

There are psychological factors that induce supervisors to create excessive organizational structures. Some supervisors, consciously or unconsciously, erect barriers between themselves and their employees because they dislike and fear the interpersonal phase of supervision. One medium-size government agency had a rigid, authoritarian structure modeled on pure classical lines. Jobs were narrowly defined, strenuous efforts were made to preserve the chain of command, and there was a multiplicity of organizational units and levels.

The agency's organizational structure seemed to produce a mass psychology on the part of supervisors in favor of erecting organizational barriers to communication. Supervisors were specialists in a technical field, and for the most part they were not too interested in their supervisory roles. As soon as they had responsibility for a group of employees, they started creating intermediate supervisory layers. One division chief with twelve employees had three subordinate supervisors, each of whom supervised three subordinates. The division chief selected as intermediate supervisors those employees whom he knew and liked, whether or not they had more knowledge or skill than the employees placed under them. As soon as these supervisors were designated, the division chief ceased having any communication with the rest of his employees. The intermediate supervisory layer acted as a bulwark between him and them. The only upward communication the employees had was with the intermediate supervisors, who reviewed and evaluated their work and made recommendations regarding promotions. This structure had a stifling effect on the initiative of the group, and the employees resented the distinctions made between them and the intermediate supervisors.

Thus we see that organization has a tremendous impact on the way work is accomplished as well as on employee performance, development, and morale and that good organization requires a high degree of both conceptual and interpersonal skill on the part of the supervisor.

3

Job Enrichment

$\mathcal{A}$s NOTED IN THE PRECEDING CHAPTER, today's employees are different from their counterparts of 25 years ago. They are better educated, they are more restless and more easily bored, and they have higher aspirations and a higher regard for their own potential. A plentiful job supply—at least for those with skills and training—has contributed greatly to employees' independence and expectations. They no longer look upon a job solely as a means of livelihood. They expect it also to provide them with satisfaction and to represent a meaningful experience in their lives. These same aspirations and expectations have now extended to the unskilled and even to the unemployed, who certainly have much less bargaining power than the trained, skilled worker; they too expect and demand jobs with meaning and a future.

Partly because of these changes in employee attitudes, partly because of the relative ease with which many routine, unskilled jobs can be automated out of existence, and partly because of recent research findings, increasing emphasis is being given to the idea of job enrichment. This notion has tremendous impact on the process of organization. It implies that good organization cannot be thought of as simply the best way of using resources to get a job done. Rather, it must be viewed as the use of resources in a way that will get the job done most effectively while at the same time providing the greatest challenge and interest to job occupants.

The Herzberg Studies

The person most responsible for advancing this concept is Dr. Frederick Herzberg of Case Western Reserve University. Herzberg and his associates conducted a series of interviews with some 200 engineers and accountants in 11 firms in the Pittsburgh area. They asked the men to recall specific incidents in their recent experience which left them with a particularly good or a particularly bad feeling about their jobs. They also asked those interviewed to indicate what effects these incidents had on their attitudes and on their performance and whether these effects were of short or long duration.[1]

The results revealed that good feelings about the jobs came when something happened which showed the men that they were doing their work particularly well or that they were becoming more expert in their professions. In

---

[1] Frederick Herzberg, et al., *Job Attitudes: Review of Research and Opinion,* Psychological Service of Pittsburgh, Pittsburgh, 1957; and Frederick Herzberg, Bernard Mausner, and B. Snyderman, *The Motivation to Work,* 2d edition, John Wiley & Sons, Inc., New York, 1959.

other words, good feelings related to the *specific tasks* the men performed rather than to such auxiliary factors as money, security, or working conditions. Bad feelings, on the other hand, usually followed some occurrence related to these auxiliary factors that made the men believe they were being treated unfairly.

The men also indicated that their job attitudes had a significant effect on the quality of their work. When they felt good about their jobs, they used more imagination, were more careful, and strove for excellence. When they felt negative about their jobs, they did not worry as much about fine details, they put less effort into their work, and they were more likely to turn in a performance that merely met minimal requirements.

Motivators Versus Hygienic Factors

The Herzberg group concluded from these interviews that two distinct sets of stimuli work to produce satisfaction or dissatisfaction with jobs. They called these stimuli *motivators* and *hygienic factors*. Motivators produce positive improvement in performance and attitudes. Hygienic factors do not produce such improvement; they merely *sustain* morale and efficiency and prevent them from deteriorating. With the engineers and accountants interviewed, the motivators—the things that produced positive job satisfaction—were opportunities to become more expert and to handle more demanding assignments. In other words, they were derived from the *job* itself. Working conditions, pay, and security did not produce *positive* satisfaction. If they were adequate, they had a neutral effect; if they were inadequate, they had a substantially negative effect on the men's attitudes and caused a rapid drop in morale and motivation. The hygienic factors created a climate in which motivators could operate.

The researchers concluded that organizations were misdirecting their efforts when they concentrated too much on such things as pay, fringe benefits, and working conditions in the belief that improvements in these factors would motivate employees to better performance. They believed also that supervisory practices were hygienic factors rather than motivators. Fair treatment and good communication did not motivate people to work harder or to like their jobs better. However, poor supervisory practices would have a negative, harmful effect on employee attitudes.

Another significant finding of these studies was the role of recognition and praise. The researchers found that these things did cause good feelings, but that the feelings lasted only a short time. Good feelings that endured were caused by such things as being assigned to stimulating work, being given considerable responsibility, and being advanced to positions of greater importance. Herzberg and his associates concluded that the key to sustained motivation is to give men assignments that push them to the limits of their abilities and continually offer them newer and greater challenge to match their growth in competence.

These findings have been criticized by other behavioral scientists, more on the basis of technicalities than on the substance of the theory. The critics have said that motivators and hygienic factors are not mutually exclusive. They have also questioned the validity of the interview method used and have claimed that the results of these interviews cannot be generalized into a theory.

The Herzberg findings do represent a rather radical departure from the human relations theories that have prevailed for many years, with their emphasis on benevolent supervisory behavior and working conditions as the prime motivator of people. Very likely Herzberg has put his finger on a most significant aspect of work that heretofore has been largely ignored—the importance of the job itself in motivating people. Perhaps this explains why the enormous amount of effort and money expended over the past 20 years on fringe benefits of all kinds, on working conditions, and on good supervisory practices has really not succeeded in motivating employees.

Two points should be kept in mind regarding the Herzberg theory. In the first place, it is complex because the motivators and hygiene factors operate simultaneously. A job may have tremendous motivating power in its opportunity for challenge and growth and achievement. It may *fail* to motivate, however, because hygienic factors are deficient. If the employee's achievements and growth are not recognized in some way, if the employee concludes that he will never be promoted no matter how much he contributes, if his efforts are ignored, or if he is treated unfairly as compared to other employees, he is likely to lose his incentive to do his best. In other words, the motivators inherent in the job become malfunctioning because of the inadequacy of hygienic factors. In some cases, the interest and challenge of the job may be strong enough to overcome the negative effects of these factors, but this is not true generally.

The converse is equally important. If a job lacks challenge and interest, if it is a dead end and affords no opportunity for growth, all the hygienic factors in the world cannot motivate the occupant to be creative or to strive continually to improve his performance. Hygienic factors, in fact, take on an exaggerated importance to employees whose jobs fail to motivate them. They become very sensitive to the attitudes and behavior of supervisors and to working conditions. A deficiency in hygienic factors can have a devastating effect on the morale and productivity of these employees.

The second point to remember about the Herzberg theory is that the men interviewed were accountants and engineers—professional employees who would be expected to have concern with work and a career. For this reason, the findings may not be applicable in the same degree to all kinds of employees. Not all employees are motivated equally by the same things. Not all employees have the same desire for achievement.

However, in the mid-1960's, Dr. Robert N. Ford of the American Telephone and Telegraph Company decided to test Herzberg's theory among blue collar and lower level white collar workers in various departments and associated companies of the Bell System. He found that Herzberg's ideas on job motivation appeared to be as valid for these employees as they were for professional people.[2]

These observations seem to indicate that it is the *job* that is the prime motivator; pay and working conditions, although important, are secondary. A perceptive supervisor who concentrates on the heart of the Herzberg findings may well have a powerful tool for motivating employees to greater accomplishment and to greater job growth and satisfaction.

The Challenge of Job Mastery

If we assume that the job is the most powerful motivator, we must identify those elements in jobs that prove

[2] *Motivation Through the Work Itself*, AMA, 1969.

to be highly satisfying and that stimulate employees to improved performance. A job, in order to be motivating, must be somewhat *beyond* an employee's present abilities and capacities. It must be a little more than he can adequately handle, yet it must be within his reach and amenable to eventual mastery. If it is so difficult that he cannot hope to master it, or if he lacks qualifications essential to the job, it will be a source of great anxiety. If he has to strive to meet the demands of the job, his greatest satisfactions will come when he sees that he *is* becoming more expert and that he has successfully accomplished a difficult part of it.

As long as he has to stretch his performance, he will be strongly motivated to conquer the job and to become its master. Once he has succeeded, the job will *cease being a motivator*. It will cease to challenge him or stimulate him to improve his performance. It may even cease to challenge him to maintain his present level of performance. This means, then, that a supervisor must *continue* to challenge an employee with increasingly difficult tasks and increasing responsibility. The supervisor's sense of timing must be good. He must perceive when the employee is ready for a further challenge. If he delays too long in offering it, the employee may lose much of his enthusiasm. If the supervisor gives the employee too many challenges at too rapid a pace before the employee is ready for them, or before he has mastered the challenge, frustration and stress may be the only results.

There is a corollary to the challenge of job mastery. There must be some recognition by the supervisor that the employee *is* becoming adept at meeting the successive demands of the job. An employee may be strongly motivated to master a job; but, if he never receives any recognition for his efforts, it is questionable that his motivation will continue. Recognition need not always be in the form of monetary reward or public praise; it may be no more than some indication, by word or deed, that the supervisor is aware of and appreciative of the employee's progress.

The essence of job enrichment, then, is (1) to make the job difficult enough to force an employee to strive and stretch his performance in order to master it and (2) to recognize the employee's accomplishments. If this is indeed the secret formula for motivation, how little supervisors understand or practice it! Organizations are full of employees whose jobs are too easy for them or who have too little to do. At the opposite extreme are organizations that have a number of employees who are unqualified or underqualified for their jobs and who, because they cannot acquire the skills and knowledge that the jobs require, either become discouraged and quit or manage to reshape the jobs to fit their own limited qualifications.

Job Enrichment and Organization

It is interesting to contrast the motivating power of self-employment or entrepreneurship with that of the same kind of work in organizations. Physicians and lawyers who are in private practice usually derive great satisfaction from their professions. This is because there is no ceiling on their growth. In fact, their professions demand continual effort to acquire greater knowledge and skill. The men are conscious of the success of their efforts when they handle a particularly difficult case successfully, or when they receive increasing recognition and respect from their colleagues, or when their practices flourish.

The job of physician or lawyer in a highly structured

organization will not have anywhere near the same degree of satisfaction unless deliberate efforts are made to provide a professional climate comparable to private practice. A physician who is assigned to do nothing but conduct preemployment medical examinations will not be greatly motivated to increase his knowledge and skill. Neither will an attorney who is assigned nothing but the preparation of briefs on one type of case. Likewise, owners of businesses usually achieve more satisfaction than does a salaried person doing similar work in an organization. This, too, is because of the open-endedness of entrepreneurship. An owner has the opportunity to improve and expand his business and develop imaginative approaches to it to the fullest extent that his abilities will allow, whereas his salaried counterpart may be severely restricted by the structure of his job and by the actions and policies of higher supervisory levels.

This brings us squarely back to the critical role of organization. The tremendous power of the job to motivate reinforces the plea of the behavioral scientists to give jobs a loose structure so that employees can grow and develop and to avoid pigeonholing people in rigid, arbitrary slots.

A loose job structure will not by itself guarantee job enrichment. As was said before, a loose structure can become a confused tangle of responsibilities and assignments, with employees not knowing what they are supposed to do and work not being done. The supervisor must play an active rather than a passive role. He must carefully structure jobs in a way that will provide the greatest challenge and development opportunities for employees. And, of great importance, he must periodically reshape the jobs if he is to provide employees with a *continuing* series of challenges. Jobs must be dynamic rather than static. This is indeed a departure from the traditional concept of jobs as stable and unchanging and from the concept that employees are carefully selected to meet the requirements of an established job. The job enrichment concept moves closer to the position that jobs may be shaped and molded by the developing abilities and skills of their occupants.

Impediments to Job Enrichment

We must recognize the fact that a number of obstacles stand in the way of this kind of ordering of jobs. Some of the impediments are institutional and beyond the control of the supervisor. Others relate directly to the way a supervisor perceives and accomplishes his job. We shall consider only those that are in the purview of the supervisor.

Structuring jobs for maximum enrichment requires a high degree of supervisory skill. The supervisor must thoroughly understand the work. He must have conceptual ability and be able to visualize the work in all its separate components, assembled in various ways. He must have imagination and a willingness to experiment. He must understand his employees equally well, and he must be able to make critical evaluations regarding their abilities and potential. He must be willing and able to delegate to subordinates as much as is feasible and to stretch himself to assume greater responsibility and be more creative in his own job. He must have enough confidence in his own capacities for growth to be willing to let go of many of his present duties, including the most challenging ones. He must enjoy personal interaction with his subordinates and must see his role as a stimulator and challenger. Finally, he must believe he has a major responsibility for the development of the people under him. Not all supervisors have these manifold abilities. In fact, we may be advocating a new breed of supervisor—one with competence and skills that have not heretofore been required.

There is another major impediment to job enrichment that is within the control of the supervisor: the practice (whether deliberate or accidental) of overstaffing. It is simply impossible to enrich jobs if there are more than enough employees to do the work. How can an employee stretch his capacity to take on other duties if those duties are already being performed by some other employee who refuses to give them up for fear that he will have nothing else to do? Any attempt at job enrichment under conditions of overstaffing will surely create jurisdictional squabbles among employees and will stir up friction and tension whose effect will be destructive.

Overstaffing is common in organizations. In some cases it is deliberate. Some supervisors consciously hire more than enough employees in order to provide a cushion against illness, absenteeism, or resignations. (Unfortunately, overstaffing frequently contributes to these things.) If work is cyclical, moving in peaks and valleys, supervisors may hire enough staff to man the peaks and then have too many people for the valleys. Frequently, better scheduling of work and of employees' working time can result in a more economical use of staff.

Much overstaffing is accidental, resulting from the supervisor's inadequate knowledge of the work or his inability to evaluate accurately the volume or the time required for various tasks. Whatever the reason, overstaffing is inimical to job enrichment. A judicious *understaffing* may well provide the best conditions for job enrichment, since it forces each employee to reach and stretch in order to get the work done.

Selection policies may be another impediment to job enrichment. Jobs cannot be enriched if the people hired for them are overqualified or temperamentally unsuited for the work. Educational and experience requirements are sometimes set too high. The personnel manager of a pharmaceutical manufacturing company with 500 employees decided to hire a person to be responsible for recruiting and employment, functions that had been taking a great deal of his own time. He established as the qualification requirements for the job a college degree in business administration and at least five years' experience in recruiting and placement. He was able to hire a man who for ten years had been in charge of college recruitment for a large paperboard company and who had lost his job as a result of a company merger and consolidation of personnel departments. He had been responsible for recruiting college graduates for technical and professional positions, as well as for executive trainee programs.

Mr. Jones, the new man, soon felt excessively restricted in duties. Most of the top executives were professional men who had been with the company for many years. They, in turn, recruited staff for the upper-level professional jobs through professional societies and through their contacts with executives in the industry. The bulk of employees were plant technicians, who were for the most part trained on the job, and clerical and office employees. Turnover was very high among both the plant technicians and the office employees, so the company was constantly recruiting locally for these jobs. The plant foremen and the office supervisors had frequent vacancies and brought continual pressure on the personnel department to recruit replacements. Mr. Jones was spending all his time telephoning various employment sources in the community and interviewing large numbers of applicants who responded to newspaper ads. Since each of the job vacancies required slightly different qualifications or experience, he could not organize any planned approach to the recruiting.

He tried to persuade the personnel manager to institute a college recruitment program as a regular source of plant technicians who could be developed for upper-level professional jobs. At the personnel manager's request he submitted a detailed, written plan, to which the personnel manager failed to respond. Then Mr. Jones began to press for authority to recruit for upper-level professional positions which the top executives were now handling personally. The personnel manager failed to act on this request also. Friction began to develop between the two men. Mr. Jones felt that his ideas were not being given any consideration, while the personnel manager believed that Mr. Jones, by pressing for more authority, was trying to usurp his job. When Mr. Jones left the company six months later there was bitter feeling on both sides.

The chances of success in this arrangement were virtually nil from the beginning. Mr. Jones was greatly over-qualified for the kind of job that existed in this company. An extensive college recruitment program was not feasible for a company of this small size with the types of jobs it had available and with the low turnover in the top ranks. The practice of having the top executives recruit the professional staff was no doubt so entrenched that the personnel manager could not have changed it, even had he wanted to. There was no way this job could have been enriched for a man of Mr. Jones's background.

The employment job would have been an ideal spot in which to train a far less qualified employee from within the company. A bright, personable clerical employee who enjoyed public contact would have been excited by the opportunity to tackle the job. She would have looked upon the constant recruiting for plant technicians and office employees as interesting and challenging and would have enjoyed the large amount of public contact involved. She would have derived satisfaction from being able to fill jobs and from working with the plant foremen and office supervisors on their vacancy problems. What was to Mr. Jones a burdensome, tedious task, which he undoubtedly felt was far below his capabilities, could have been to a far less qualified person a rich, rewarding job full of challenge and satisfaction.

Large organizations and government agencies often recruit college graduates and then place them in routine clerical jobs that could be performed by individuals with no college training. This is a practice that makes job enrichment impossible.

The temperamental requirements of jobs are as important as the educational and experiential requirements. People vary greatly in the kinds of work they enjoy the most and perform the best. Selling and bookkeeping, for example, are kinds of work requiring totally different temperaments. An active, restless person who enjoys variety and dealing with people and who is aggressive and competitive would probably make a good salesman but would be unable to adjust to the slow pace and detail of bookkeeping. Similarly, a person who is excellent at detail and is happy sitting at a desk all day doing repetitive work would probably be a good bookkeeper (if he had an aptitude for numbers) but would lack the drive and competitiveness and perhaps the gift of gab to succeed at selling.

Temperament would be of prime importance in the employment job that was just described. Any person selected as a trainee for the job should be bright and person-able and should enjoy working with people. She should also be quick in moving from one task to another and be able to accomplish her work in spite of repeated interruptions. She would probably be an employee who was not happy doing routine, repetitive clerical work. Many clerical employees would be temperamentally unsuited for the employment job. The constant interruptions would be utterly frustrating to them, as would the incessant pressure to fill vacancies. They would be unable to keep track of all the details of the job or to follow through on things because of the distractions. Such employees would be much better suited to a structured type of work, where duties were clear-cut and where the employees could work at a steady pace on the same task until it was completed.

Finally, the work itself may be a major impediment to job enrichment. Obviously some types of jobs can be enriched more easily than others. Some jobs by their nature have built-in enrichment, and the supervisor's main concern should be to avoid erecting structural and organizational barriers that would destroy the inherent interest and challenge of the jobs. On the other hand, some work is just plain monotonous, and there is little a supervisor can do to make it otherwise. His best bet is to try to find employees whose temperaments are most compatible with this type of work and then rely on hygienic factors to maintain their morale.

Dynamic Versus Static Work Situations

Organizing jobs for maximum enrichment is much easier in a dynamic situation, where the work itself is changing and the organization is growing, than it is in a static situation. The research and development case that was described in the preceding chapter is a good example of a dynamic work situation. The unit was growing and the work was constantly changing as new projects and studies were undertaken. Moreover, a variety of skills and backgrounds could be employed in the various parts of the work, since it ranged from pure research to product development and testing. The work had a great deal of built-in interest and challenge so long as the supervisor did not destroy them by introducing too much structure and too many supervisory levels or by employing the wrong types of people or the wrong mix of skills and background.

If the supervisor used an unstructured form of organization, with temporary task groups established to undertake particular projects, it would be essential that he employ individuals who were temperamentally suited for that climate. They should be people who thrive on variety and change, who enjoy the challenge of continually tackling new problems, and who can make an easy transition from one project or task to another. The plan would fail if the supervisor hired people who want and need clear guidelines or who perform best when they know exactly what is expected of them and what they will be doing from day to day.

New organizations or organizational units that are growing and expanding or changing in functions, programs, or objectives have a dynamic quality. Older, more stable organizations may acquire this quality if they undertake new programs or make significant changes in their operational methods.

Change is the hallmark of today's world. For that reason, dynamic work situations are very common today. Most private businesses and industries are undergoing continual change. Manufacturing processes are being automated; new methods of marketing and distributing goods are evolving; there is a continuous stream of new products. Mergers are frequent, and many companies are diversifying into different and often totally unrelated product lines. Many service industries are changing with the same rapidity. The hospital, nursing, and medical fields are undergoing revolutionary change, resulting both from scientific and technological advances and from increasing demands of government and the public for improved and expanded health care. Government at all levels is in a period of drastic change, as it strives to cope with new problems and with demands for increased or totally new services.

Unfortunately, many supervisors who are intimately involved with this process of change have responded to and been concerned with the *problems* it has brought, but they have not been sufficiently alert to the enormous *potential* it has for job enrichment. Many supervisors have vitiated this great potential by insisting on old, authoritarian forms of job structure and organization and by attempting to apply these forms to situations for which they are no longer appropriate.

Static Work Situations

Many kinds of work are static; that is, they remain very much the same over a period of time. Nevertheless, they may consist of a range of tasks from the relatively uncomplicated to the complex and difficult. These work situations require that a supervisor use an entirely different approach to job enrichment. Much skilled and semiskilled factory work is of this nature, as is much selling and administration. Most clerical work is of this type, in-

cluding such routine tasks as filing and card punching. For
the most part this work requires a good deal of job structure in order to meet demands of production or time deadlines. A supervisor can best provide for job enrichment
by giving employees an opportunity to learn and undertake increasingly difficult tasks.

The most common approach to organizing work with
a range of difficulty is to slice it vertically, with different
employees performing tasks of different levels of difficulty. This process may be shown as follows:

Most difficult	—Employee G
Moderately difficult	—Employees E and F
Simplest	—Employees A, B, C, and D

The newest, most unskilled, most inexperienced employees are assigned to the simplest tasks; those with
greater ability and experience are assigned the moderately
difficult tasks, while the most difficult tasks are given to
the most competent and experienced employee.

If a supervisor has made the right judgment as to employees' abilities, this is an efficient way of organizing
work. It makes good use of experience and abilities; it will
produce a good volume of work; it is economical from the
standpoint of cost, assuming that employees are paid according to the gradations of job difficulty. It also provides
an orderly mechanism for training employees in the more
difficult tasks. The arrangement will no doubt work well
if there is a reasonable amount of turnover, so that employees on the lower rungs have good reason to hope they
can move into the higher bracket as soon as they have acquired enough skill. However, if turnover is too low to
permit the upward movement of employees on the lower
rung as soon as they have acquired the necessary experience and skill, this divison of the work will establish a

ceiling on employees' progress. The more experienced and capable employees who are still performing the simplest tasks will soon become dissatisfied. The supervisor could provide much more job enrichment by organizing the work in this manner:

Most difficult
Moderately difficult } —Employees C, D, E, F, and G
Simplest

Simplest   —Employees A and B

Under this arrangement the newest, most inexperienced employees (A and B) would still be assigned only the simplest tasks for as long a period as necessary to master them. After this initial period of training, all employees would perform a mix of tasks of varying degrees of difficulty: some of the simplest, some of the moderately difficult, and some of the most difficult.

No matter how the supervisor organizes the work, the time will come when an employee will outgrow the duties of his job. This situation presents the supervisor with a very difficult problem when the work is static and there are no more higher-level duties for the employee to undertake. One thing that might be done is to have him learn other jobs even if these jobs are on the same relative level of difficulty. If the supervisor has no jobs under his jurisdiction that would be appropriate, he might work with fellow supervisors or with his personnel department to arrange a temporary outside assignment for his employee or possibly arrange a temporary exchange of employees.

Most employees are motivated and interested as long as they are learning something new and striving to become proficient in a new job. Switching employees to other jobs, however, must be handled with great care. It is a policy that is generally more appropriate for higher-level administrative employees than for clerical or semiskilled staff. Some clerical employees would welcome the chance to learn a new job in another organizational unit, whereas some employees prefer the security of remaining on a job whose duties they know perfectly.

The supervisor should thoroughly discuss any idea of job movement with the employee before making arrangements for another assignment. He should be sure the employee wants to make the change and understands that its purpose is his own development. Any such assignment should be arranged only *after* the employee has mastered all possible tasks of his own job and has, in fact, outgrown them. When an employee is assigned to learn a new job, he should be given full responsibility for it and made accountable for results. He should not be assigned to it merely as a trainee or observer.

A practice of moving employees horizontally into other jobs of the same relative level is an excellent means of broadening and developing individuals in administrative staff positions. Many organizations make a definite separation of the staff offices of personnel management, budget and finance, and the like. Staff members assigned to these various functions normally move in a strictly vertical line within their particular specialty. Once they have learned and become proficient in the duties of a specialty, they would benefit from being assigned to one of the other specialties for a specific duration. As an example, personnel specialists might move into budget and finance positions and remain there until they have learned the work and become proficient in it. They should also be required to supplement work experience with outside courses in budgeting or accounting. Such a practice would not only provide greater job challenge and interest; it would also produce broader and more capable employees.

There are some kinds of work that simply cannot be enriched beyond a certain point. Manual, unskilled work usually remains the same day after day. Very little can be done to introduce greater interest or challenge into such jobs as janitor or maid. Many materials-handling or warehousing jobs are routine and unvaried, as are the jobs of laborers, messengers, deliverymen, or operators of simple duplicating equipment such as copying or mimeographing machines. The supervisor of this kind of work would be wise not to try to enrich such jobs. Above all, he should not try to introduce some artificial factor of decision making or responsibility that the employees will readily recognize as phony. His best efforts should go into making sure that he does not place on these routine jobs employees who are temperamentally unsuited for them and who have the potential for work that is much more demanding mentally. He should also be sure that the hygienic factors of pay, working conditions, and good supervision are adequate.

The Role of Job Evaluation

Job evaluation is closely related to the way work is organized, and it can have a major impact on a supervisor's efforts to enrich jobs. Most large private organizations and government agencies have some system of job evaluation. Supervisors do not need to know all the technical details and fine points of the system, but they should understand the basic concepts underlying job evaluation and the way it affects the supervisory job.

Job evaluation is purely and simply a tool for managerial control. It is a method of evaluating and grading or ranking *jobs* rather than evaluating or ranking their occupants. The duties and responsibilities of the job itself control its ranking, rather than the experience, ability, or quality of performance of the person doing the job. Its primary purpose is to measure the monetary worth (in the form of salary or wages) of a job or group of jobs and to maintain control over the amount paid for the various kinds of work performed. A secondary purpose is to spell out the skills, abilities, and other qualifications required to perform the jobs. In the public service, job evaluation is also used to establish avenues or ladders of promotion.

It is not the function of a job evaluation system to determine *what* the content of jobs should be or how jobs should be organized; that is the function of supervisors. Job evaluation comes *after* jobs have been organized and structured, and it measures jobs as they *are* rather than as they should be. The basic medium of job evaluation is the job description, which should accurately describe the salient features of the jobs. Descriptions are prepared (depending upon the policy of the organization) by employees, by supervisors, or by job analysts after discussion with the employee and his supervisor.

Job Evaluation Systems

There are two broad types of job evaluation systems: point evaluation, widely used in industry, and position classification, most widely used in the public service. In both systems, the various components of jobs are analyzed and measured against predetermined factors or characteristics.

The starting point in establishing a job evaluation system is to decide on the factors to be used to measure jobs and then to differentiate several *degrees* of each factor, as illustrated in the following simplified example:

Factor	*Degrees*		
	(1)	(2)	(3)
Difficulty and complexity of work; skills and knowledge required	Simple; can be learned in brief training period	Moderate; requires several years of experience	Very complex; requires college education or equivalent

In *point evaluation systems*, a numerical value is assigned to each degree of each factor. In any system, great attention must be paid to the factors used and to their gradations. These factors and degrees of difficulty must be clearly delineated and distinguished from one another (in much more detail than shown in the example just given). They must be described in writing so that there will be as little room for misinterpretation as possible. In point evaluation systems, these definitions are set forth in a manual to be used by the job analysts, who compare all jobs to the standards and assign a total numerical value or score to the job. Some systems—called *weighted-in-money-systems*—equate the total score with actual pay; for example, a total score of 450 equals a salary of $450. This system is very cumbersome in a period of frequent change in salary scales and is little used today. It is more common for the total score or range of scores assigned to jobs to correspond to a pay *grade*; that is, job values of 400–499 correspond to Pay Grade 6, which has a current salary range of $500 to $625 a month.

Numerical scores or values are not used in *position*

classification systems. Instead, the different degrees of the various factors used are delineated in the form of class specifications or standards, which describe prototype jobs that are typical of the class. It is essential that the class specifications clearly state which factors are most important to the class and the degrees to which these factors are present. Many different jobs could fall into the same class. Furthermore, a single occupational category might contain several different classes, each representing different levels of difficulty and responsibility and each commanding different pay scales. For example, accountants may be in any of four classes depending upon the difficulty and complexity of the work: junior accountant, intermediate accountant, senior accountant, and principal accountant. Some organizations may designate these classes as Accountants I, II, III, and IV. When this is the case, the specifications must unmistakably differentiate each class from the others by describing the degree to which various factors are present.

The factors against which jobs are evaluated may differ between point evaluation and position classification systems. Working conditions, physical demands, hazards, and responsibility for the safety of others are usually given more consideration in point evaluation systems used in industrial plants. Most systems (both point evaluation and position classification) generally use variations of the following factors: difficulty and complexity of work; variety of assignments; knowledge and skills required; responsibility for the work of others, for independent actions or decisions, for programs, methods, or policies, for public contacts, or for the lives of others; seriousness and consequence of errors; originality of thinking required; and supervision and guides over the work.

Relation of Classification and Pay

As noted earlier, the primary purpose of job evaluation is to establish the money value of jobs. Any number of jobs that are considered to be of equal worth, although they may represent many different occupations, are grouped into a series of pay grades. There are two major considerations in establishing a pay grade. One is internal consistency. Equal pay for equal work is a cardinal principle of job evaluation. Jobs having approximately equal levels of difficulty and responsibility and approximately equal qualification requirements should have equal pay grades. The job evaluation system must maintain this equity among jobs as far as possible.

The other consideration in establishing pay scales is that the pay plan must reflect prevailing wages in the community in order to attract employees to work in the organization. These two considerations frequently conflict with each other. Prevailing wages for a particular occupation are determined by labor market supply and demand, by the degree to which the occupation is unionized, and by other variables, rather than strictly by the level of difficulty and the qualification requirements of the work. The contrast in pay between highly unionized crafts such as plumbers and carpenters and largely non-union professions such as teachers and librarians illustrates the compelling force of prevailing wages. When there is a conflict between internal consistency of the job evaluation system and prevailing wages, it is the latter that must take precedence simply because of the imperative need to recruit qualified personnel.

Supervisors should learn the basic features of any job evaluation plan in use in their organizations. They should understand the factors and degrees against which jobs are measured, and they should know what determines whether a job falls into one grade level or the next. They should know how to prepare concise and succinct job descriptions that set forth the essential elements of the jobs. They should know what effect their method of organizing the work will have on the grade level of the respective jobs. Generally speaking, the more difficult, complex, and varied an employee's duties are and the more responsibility he has for independent action, the higher the grade level of his job will be.

Job Evaluation and Job Enrichment

Job evaluation is a product of the classical theories of organization. For that reason, it is biased in favor of structured jobs with clearly defined duties and responsibilities. Most job evaluation systems presuppose that work will be so organized that individual jobs will contain duties that are all at much the same level of difficulty (or at the same degree of the factors used for measuring jobs). If jobs do contain duties that are at different levels of difficulty, the systems presuppose that one level will clearly occupy the major part of the incumbent's working time. In this kind of job mix, it becomes necessary for the analyst to try to measure the percentage of time spent on various levels of work.

Let us consider again the example that was used previously, showing two different ways of organizing work that contains duties ranging from the simplest to the most difficult. (See Exhibit 1.)

The old plan divides the work into very clear-cut jobs for evaluation purposes. If the three levels of work differ markedly from one another, the jobs probably will fall

Exhibit 1

Old Plan		New Plan	
Level of Work	No. of Employees	Level of Work	No. of Employees
Most difficult	1	Most difficult	
		Moderately difficult	} 5
Moderately difficult	2	Simplest	
Simplest	4	Simplest	2
	7		7

into three classes or grades, each of which will carry a different pay scale. Assuming that these are clerical jobs, those that contain the simplest duties might be junior clerks; those with the moderately difficult duties, senior clerks; and the one job with the most difficult tasks, a principal clerk.

The new plan of organization presents an entirely different job evaluation problem. Five employees are now performing a mix of duties that ranges from the simplest to the most difficult, while two employees are performing only the simplest tasks. The two jobs containing only the simplest tasks would continue to be classed as junior clerks. But the five jobs containing a mix of difficulty present a problem in job evaluation. The job analyst would have to determine what percentage of time each of the five clerks devoted to tasks on the different levels.

This percentage can be estimated because it is known how many man-hours were devoted daily to the three levels of difficulty under the old plan, when the jobs were strictly segregated by level. The contrast between the old and new plans in the man-hours allocated to the different tasks is shown in Exhibit 2.

Exhibit 2

	Old Plan		New Plan	
Level of Work	Employees	Man-Hours	Employees	Man-Hours
Most difficult	1	8	—	—
Moderately difficult	2	16	—	—
Simplest	4	32	2	16
Mix of all three levels	—	—	5	40
	7	56	7	56

After subtracting the 16 man-hours (two employees) devoted only to the simplest tasks, under the new plan the five jobs containing a mix of all three levels would contain man-hours on each level as shown in Exhibit 3.

The three different levels of work would probably be distributed evenly among the five employees. They would devote 20 percent of their time to the most difficult tasks, 40 percent to the moderately difficult, and 40 percent to the simplest. Under most job evaluation plans, all five jobs would be allocated to the job grade equivalent to the senior clerk level. The jobs are above the

Exhibit 3

Level of Work	Man-Hours	Percent of Total	Job Grade Level
Most difficult	8	20	Principal clerk
Moderately difficult	16	40	Senior clerk
Simplest (32 minus 16)	16	40	Junior clerk
	40	100	

junior clerk level, since 60 percent of total time is devoted to duties at the moderately difficult and most difficult levels. The jobs could not be allocated to the principal clerk grade because only 20 percent of time is devoted to work of that level.

The effect of the new plan of organizing the work on the evaluation of the jobs is an important consideration. The new method, in fact, might be a mixed blessing. Two employees who would otherwise be stuck at the junior clerk level could move up to senior clerk and at the same time perform more varied and interesting work. On the other hand, the senior clerk grade would be a ceiling. No one could move up to principal clerk unless the work were resegregated strictly by level of difficulty.

Thus job enrichment cannot be expected to solve all work problems in every situation. But it can help an imaginative supervisor to smooth out some of the difficulties.

4

Planning and Scheduling

$\mathcal{P}$LANNING MAY BE HIGHLY COMPLEX AND SO-phisticated. Large corporations frequently devote an entire department to it. This kind of planning usually is long range and includes forecasts of sales, economic and market conditions, capital expenditures, and new product development.

Planning may also be simple and unspecialized, and this is the kind that is of most value to the supervisor. It is short range and operational. It consists primarily of visualizing the many steps that make up an operation and preparing so that the operation itself can be performed quickly and efficiently. Scheduling is a closely related function. Planning might be considered the advance thinking about the multiple aspects of the work, while scheduling consists of translating these thoughts into sequential steps to which time limits are assigned. Planning is often described as the process of asking the questions what, why, when, who, and how. Scheduling might be described as the process of supplying detailed answers to those questions.

Using Planning and Scheduling

The dual processes of planning and scheduling have reached their zenith in manufacturing industries. Orderly manufacturing requires the precise meshing of multiple steps and operations. The time factor is crucial, since the deadline for the finished product can be met only if time intervals for the many intermediate steps are accurately established and met.

Large manufacturing firms usually centralize their planning and scheduling operations into a production control or production planning department, which has responsibility for planning and scheduling production orders from the requisitioning of raw materials through the various manufacturing processes to the final assembly and inspection. These departments have responsibility for controlling the entire manufacturing flow, and they have authority to step into any organizational unit to expedite the work or to insure that deadlines are being met. Because of the complexity of the production process and the many different departments involved, detailed written plans, schedules, and orders are essential.

A centralized system of production planning and scheduling of the kind just described limits the plant foreman's responsibility. He does not have to coordinate the flow of raw materials or the sequential completion of totally different manufacturing processes. He does, however, have to plan and schedule the work of his own employees and his own machines in order to meet the production deadline given him. He must anticipate various possible breakdowns in machines or the illness, accident, or termination of employees. He must have contingency plans for handling these potential disruptions to production. For example, he should train several employees in the operation of each essential machine. And he should decide in advance where it might be possible to double up by having an employee run two machines or by taking an employee off some other work temporarily in order to have him man a machine.

The foremen should have plans for preventing machine breakdown, as far as possible, by establishing a regular schedule of oiling, cleaning, and inspection. Of course, this kind of planning and scheduling is far simpler than controlling an entire production process. The foreman can carry many of his plans in his head without the need for developing elaborate written plans and schedules.

It is in fact somewhat surprising that techniques that have proved so successful in manufacturing have made such tiny inroads into nonmanufacturing enterprises. Yet the fact is most service industries and government have not begun to tap the enormous potential of good planning and scheduling. Many supervisors have never thought of planning and scheduling as one of their major responsibilities. They respond to events instead of trying to control them. In this respect, they are slaves of the work they supervise rather than its masters.

Many service industries could reap huge benefits from the proper use of planning and scheduling techniques. Hospitals and related health institutions could be major beneficiaries. It is interesting to speculate on what might happen to the quality of hospital care and to hospital costs if all hospital supervisors understood and applied these techniques. Many small businesses, such as building trades contractors, could profit from better planning and scheduling. Government at all levels offers a vast untapped field for improved efficiency with the use of these methods.

A supervisor should know *how* to use these techniques and *when* to use them. Nothing is more wasteful or more confusing than for supervisors to attempt to use techniques for their own sake or because they think it is the modern or sophisticated thing to do. Any technique will produce benefits only if it is appropriate to a particular situation. Planning and scheduling should be used only if they can bring order and control to a situation that otherwise would be unmanageable.

A supervisor of routine, repetitive work has no need to spend a lot of time on planning and scheduling. Most of the planning that is necessary for relatively uncomplicated work can be done mentally. It would be foolish for a factory foreman in a situation where planning and control were centralized to develop detailed, written plans and schedules.

Two kinds of work situations are most responsive to planning and scheduling: (1) work that has a time deadline and requires the coordination and completion of multiple intermediate steps, either simultaneously or sequentially; and (2) work that moves in cycles, with distinct peaks and valleys of volume. We shall discuss some examples of each of these types of work and ways in which planning and scheduling might be applied to them. But first we should consider the techniques themselves.

We have already said that planning consists of thinking through all of the many steps that make up a complete operation, and scheduling consists of translating these thoughts into specific steps to which time limits are assigned. Scheduling can apply to the work itself, or it can apply to the working hours and job assignments of employees. Work that is cyclical may not be amenable to a kind of scheduling that would smooth out the peaks and troughs. In such cases, employees' work schedules should be arranged so as to provide maximum staff coverage for the peaks without overstaffing during the low-volume periods.

The Gantt Chart

A very simple device for planning and scheduling work is the Gantt Chart (shown in Exhibit 4), developed by Henry L. Gantt, one of the pioneers in the scientific management movement. It is easy to use and is adequate for all but the most complex scheduling problems. It shows the operational steps along the vertical axis and the completion dates (both planned and actual) along the horizontal axis. Its greatest advantage is the graphic way in which it shows whether each step is on schedule. Modifications of the Gantt Chart may be used to depict the cyclical flow of work or to schedule the working hours of employees to meet the needs of cyclical variations in volume.

There are a number of commercial versions of the Gantt Chart, particularly the Produc-trol Board and the Sched-U-Graph. The principal feature of each is visual control. Supervisors who have fairly complex or repeti-

Exhibit 4

THE GANTT CHART

Operational Steps		Completion Date												
		1	2	3	4	5	6	7	8	9	10	11	12	13
1.	Planned	– – – – – – – – – – – –												
	Actual													
2.	Planned	– – – – – – – – – – –												
	Actual													
3.	Planned													
	Actual													
4.	Planned													
	Actual													
5.	Planned													
	Actual													
6.	Planned													
	Actual													
7.	Planned													
	Actual													

tive planning and scheduling problems should investigate these and other commercial devices.

Increasingly, the most difficult planning and scheduling problems are being handled by computers. However, problems of this complexity are usually beyond the responsibility of the average supervisor and probably should be centralized under a specialized department. Any work that requires a large amount of coordination among different organizational units can best be scheduled and controlled on a centralized basis.

Work Involving Deadlines and Multiple Steps

A social science research study is an example of the kind of work that needs to be carefully planned and scheduled. Data must be obtained from a variety of sources. Then the data must be analyzed and interpreted, and an analytical report must be written. A number of different operational steps go into the study, each of which must be completed before the next step can begin. If there is any kind of deadline for the final report, the supervisor *has* to plan and schedule the work, unless he is willing to risk having inadequate data or unless he is willing to miss the deadline because the study is incomplete.

The planning process consists of the supervisor's asking himself the following questions: What is the deadline for the final report? What data do we need? Where and how shall we get the information? If we use primary sources, how should we design our sample? How much time will be required to obtain the data? What deadlines should be set for completion of the data collection phase? How much time should be allowed for tabulation and analysis? How much time is needed for writing and reviewing the final report? What staff should be assigned to the various parts of the study? What other organizational units will be involved? What discussions should be held with them and when? How can progress be measured? A supervisor should develop answers to all of these questions and should schedule the various steps *before* he begins the study.

Assume that the supervisor decided to conduct a pilot study, obtaining data from five primary sources selected from a stratified sample. First he determined that 30 days would be allowed for completion of the entire study, including the writing of a final report on the findings. Then he decided which staff members he would assign to the study, and he planned the time requirements for the different steps involved. He calculated that three days would be required to design the survey questionnaire. He met with the head of the printing unit and obtained his commitment to print the questionnaire in one day. Allowing an extra day as a margin of safety, he assigned a total of five days to the designing and printing of the questionnaire. His assistant, Brown, would be given the responsibility for that function while the supervisor selected the sample and wrote a letter to each of the five sources, explaining the purpose of the study and requesting their cooperation.

The letters to the five sources would accompany the questionnaire and would be mailed as soon as the questionnaires were printed. Ten days would be allowed for return of completed questionnaires. (The sources contacted were requested to return them in a week, leaving three extra days as a margin of safety.) Two days would be required for tabulating and summarizing the data. The supervisor also met with the head of computer services and made arrangements to have the work done at the specified time.

Two clerks would then edit and review the data and prepare tables, using a format to be designed by the assistant, Brown, while he waited for the data to be received. Two days were set aside for this step. Brown would then interpret the data and write a final report. Five days would be allowed for writing and typing, two more days would be provided for review and approval by the supervisor, and another day would be reserved for the final typing. If all the steps were completed on schedule, the study would be finished three days ahead of the thirty-day deadline.

Exhibit 5 shows the various steps and their starting and completion dates plotted on a Gantt Chart. A great advantage in the Gantt Chart is that it forces a supervisor to break down the total job into its various components and requires him to schedule starting and completion dates for each. In the case just described, the supervisor did a good job of planning the various steps required to complete the study. He showed foresight when he discussed his project in advance with the heads of both the printing unit and computer services and arranged with them to have the work done on a scheduled date. If he had merely sent the printing unit a questionnaire with the request that it be printed as a rush job, that unit would probably have added it to all of its other "rush" jobs and completed it when it had the time. If he had waited until he had received all of the data and had then asked the head of computer services to process the material immediately, he might have found that other rush jobs had preempted all computer time for several days. Frustration and probably ill feelings on both sides were prevented by the supervisor's advance planning and advance consultation with other organizational units.

The other major advantage of the Gantt Chart is its visual control of progress. Each completed operation is plotted on the chart opposite the word *actual,* so that progress may be compared with the planned completion dates. In Exhibit 5, we see that operations one and two were finished on schedule, but that the data collection fell far behind. Sources A and B sent their data in ahead of time. Source E returned his data at the end of the ten days allowed on the schedule. Source C was on vacation when the letter and questionnaire were received and was, therefore, three days behind schedule in returning the information. Source D was way behind schedule. The

Exhibit 5

USE OF THE GANTT CHART TO PLAN AND SCHEDULE A SOCIAL SCIENCE RESEARCH STUDY

Operational Steps		Completion Dates — Month of March (1–31)
1. Design and print survey questionnaires. (Brown)	Planned / Actual	
2. Select sample; write letters to sources; type.	Planned / Actual	
3. Request data from sources and receive data.	A Planned / Actual, B Planned / Actual	
4. Plan format of tables and final report while waiting for data. (Brown)	C Planned / Actual, D Planned / Actual, E Planned / Actual	
5. Tabulate and summarize data. (Computer Services)	Planned / Actual	
6. Review and edit data; prepare tables. (Clerks Smith & Jones)	Planned / Actual	
7. Interpret data; write report. (Brown)	Planned / Actual	
8. Review and approve report; final typing.	Planned / Actual	

original source D refused to participate in the survey and another one had to be selected from the sample and contacted.

Since the data could not be tabulated and summarized until all five sources had responded, it was nearly impossible for the supervisor to complete this project and have a final report prepared in 30 days. The chart alerted him to trouble and he had to decide whether to go ahead with the remaining steps as planned, thus permitting the study to be finished behind schedule, or whether to apply extra effort and staff to the remaining steps in order to meet the 30-day deadline.

The flaw in planning in this case was the failure to allow enough time for the data collection in case of refusals or other unforeseen events. Perhaps additional time should have been allowed for a preliminary contact of the five sources, in order to make sure they would participate before mailing them the questionnaires.

The study just described is a typical planning and scheduling problem. It is straightforward, and the work moves in a linear, sequential fashion. The supervisor has a great deal of control over the operational steps necessary to accomplish the job as well as over the time schedules established. Plans have to be coordinated with other organizational units (printing and computer services), and all of the operational steps must be meshed together in the proper sequence and completed at the right time. If completion of any step falls behind, the remaining schedule must be adjusted, or extra effort must be applied to the successive steps in order to adhere to the original time schedule.

Many other types of work can be made more manageable and can be performed more efficiently by good planning and scheduling techniques. The supervisor of a large print shop, for example, should carefully plan and schedule the work so that it moves through the various production steps without delay or interruption in order that deadlines can be established and adhered to. The supervisor of a large computer programming section that handles a heavy volume and wide variety of programs can achieve much greater control and efficiency by "programming" his own work. The supervisor of computer operations needs to plan and schedule his work so that the numerous programs flow in an orderly fashion through the various processes from key punching to computer processing.

Any kind of building trades contracting work is a prime candidate for planning and scheduling techniques. The work of several different crafts, such as brick or cement masons, carpenters, plumbers, and electricians, must be coordinated and timed so that it is performed in the proper sequence and according to a predetermined time schedule. Materials have to be ordered and delivered if the work is to proceed without delay. The general lack of good planning and scheduling in this field—especially among small contractors—can be attested to by anyone who has endured the frustration of having a house built or remodeled. There are often countless delays while waiting for materials to be delivered or for a subcontractor or various craftsmen to complete their part of the work before the job can proceed.

Many kinds of clerical work can be accomplished more efficiently and with less effort and stress through good planning and scheduling. Work that involves the reviewing and processing of a heavy volume of documents or orders should be planned and scheduled if a number of employees are engaged in the operations.

All of the work just described has several things

in common. A prime objective in each case has been to accomplish an orderly, progressive flow of work toward an ultimate end with the least amount of interruption and delay. The work has consisted of multiple steps that must be performed either sequentially or simultaneously before the rest of the work can proceed. A number of different people, and in some cases different organizational units, perform these steps, and their efforts have to be coordinated. Finally, a major objective in each case is completion of the work by a certain time.

Work That Is Cyclical

In contrast, work whose volume consists of peaks and troughs presents the supervisor with quite a different planning and scheduling problem. The first decision he should make is whether it is possible to smooth out the irregular volume. Some cyclical work can be controlled, at least partially, by scheduling. Some hospital operations are of this nature. For example, a hospital admitting office has a very heavy workload in the afternoon. Many admitting supervisors make a practice of asking all patients to come in at the same time (such as at 2:00 or 3:00 p.m.) or within a short time interval (such as from 2:00 to 4:00 p.m.). Patients cannot be admitted until rooms are ready, and this factor is influenced by the hospital discharge hour. The admitting office supervisor, however, can smooth out the heavy peak and eliminate excessive patient waiting by making definite appointments every 15 minutes or every half-hour, depending upon the time required for the admission procedures and the cushion of extra time that should be allowed for emergencies.

Outpatient clinics frequently follow the same practice of asking all patients to come at the same time and then to wait their turn (which sometimes can mean several hours of waiting). A more efficient work plan—and certainly one more acceptable to patients—would be to schedule definite appointments in order to stagger the influx. Nursing units have traditionally had a heavy volume of work in midmorning and then a sharp drop-off. This cycle has resulted in very high costs because the units are staffed for the high-volume period and the personnel are underemployed for a good part of their working shift. This peak can be smoothed out substantially by departing from the nursing tradition of morning care, which requires that each patient be given his bath and have his bed linens changed the first thing in the morning. Many hospital operations could be made more efficient by the use of planning and scheduling techniques.

Businesses serving the public have attempted to smooth out peaks by charging lower prices during off days and hours. Airlines, for example, give a discount on transcontinental flights that are begun and ended during low-traffic periods. Retail establishments of various kinds schedule sales or give price discounts during off periods.

However, there is a point beyond which a supervisor cannot go in smoothing out peaks and troughs of work. The hospital admitting supervisor can modify the work cycle, but she cannot eliminate it altogether. And some cycles cannot be modified at all. Restaurants, for example, cannot change the mealtime eating habits of the public. In these cases, the supervisor should understand the work cycle, anticipate the peak hours, and prepare in advance for them as much as possible. Then he should schedule the working hours of his employees, so that he has maximum staff available for the high-volume period without being overstaffed for the remainder of the day.

Advance preparation can be the key to efficient handling of work that has a high-volume peak. It is essential that a restaurant prepare as much food as possible before the rush hour starts. Vegetables must be cleaned and prepared, salads and desserts made, bread and butter put out, creamers and sugar bowls filled, and as much cooking done as possible.

One of the keys to an efficient hospital admitting office is preplanning and advance preparation of as much of the work as possible. Preadmission information should be obtained from patients before they arrive. Other keys to efficiency are scheduling the arrival of nonemergency admissions at appointed times and arranging employees' working days and hours to meet the peak periods.

The supervisor of a busy hospital admitting office received constant complaints from patients and their physicians about the excessive time spent waiting after the patients had arrived at the admitting office. She had a staff of eight employees, including herself, for seven-day coverage of the day and evening shifts. All day-shift employees worked from 7:00 a.m. to 3:30 p.m., while the evening-shift staff worked from 3:00 p.m. to 11:30 p.m.

Instead of hiring additional employees, the supervisor made a complete analysis of the work of the office and the procedures used. She discovered that her present staff could handle the workload and that patient waits could be held to a minimum if she made certain basic changes in planning and scheduling. She began a vigorous preadmissions program; nearly all essential information was obtained from the patient before the day of admission and all paperwork was prepared before the patient's arrival. This change shortened the average time required for an interview from 30 minutes to 10 minutes.

Previously, all patients had been asked to come in at 2:00 p.m. She found that giving them definite appointment times would smooth out the workload and prevent the simultaneous arrival of many patients. By analyzing the daily admissions over a period of weeks, she obtained a better understanding of the variations in staff coverage required for different days. She found that she could make maximum staff available at the times when it was most needed by staggering the employees' working hours and by making some adjustments in the days they worked. Exhibit 6 shows her use of a modified Gantt Chart to plot staff coverage for the heavy admission days, Monday through Thursday.

Exhibit 6

MODIFIED GANTT CHART SHOWING STAFF COVERAGE OF HOSPITAL ADMITTING OFFICE

	Monday through Thursday	
	Hours of Work	
Employee	A.M. 7 8 9 10 11 12	P.M. 1 2 3 4 5 6 7 8 9 10 11
Employee A	— — — — — — — — — —	
Supervisor	— — — — — — — — — — —	
Employee B	— — — — — — — — — — —	
Employee C	— — — — — — — — — —	
Employee D	— — — — — — — — — —	
Employee E	— — — — — — — — — —	
Employee F	— — — — — — — — — — —	

Fluctuating and Unpredictable Work

The most difficult kind of work to plan and schedule is that having highly fluctuating and sometimes erratic volume, determined by external factors beyond the control of the supervisor. Nearly all kinds of emergency work are of this nature. The emergency room of a hospital has no control over its volume, any more than an ambulance service or a rescue squad does. Supervisors of these functions frequently learn from experience when to anticipate heavy volume, and they brace themselves for it. For example, an emergency room or an ambulance service usually can expect more calls over holidays or long holiday weekends. Supervisors of these units should have plans for all eventualities. They obviously cannot be staffed completely for everything that could happen, but they do need to have contingency plans and procedures for calling on reserve forces if there should be overwhelming emergencies.

Some supervisors are confronted with two kinds of work simultaneously. Part of the work may progress steadily and be amenable to planning and control, but at the same time there are frequent interruptions by unplanned situations that require immediate attention. A plumbing contractor, for example, has installation work that he can plan and schedule, but at the same time he receives frequent calls for emergency repairs. Maintenance units have similar problems. It is very difficult to schedule employees to handle both kinds of work, since the service calls by their nature create inefficiency. If the volume of service calls is low, the supervisor can probably plan and schedule the installation work and then pull men off temporarily to answer service calls. If this happens often, however, it can completely disrupt any scheduled work and it is very upsetting and frustrating to most employees. The supervisor may have no choice but to assign a man or a crew as trouble shooters, whose sole duties are to answer service calls, and simply accept the built-in inefficiency of idle time between calls. At least this way he can keep the installation work progressing on schedule.

Many clerical functions that serve the public have the same characteristic of partially static and partially erratic volume. Employees may have routine work to perform, which they may have to interrupt to wait on customers. Many cashiering jobs have this feature, as do clerical jobs in real estate, insurance offices, and many government offices serving the public. The combination of routine work and public contact can be handled without difficulty by most clerks. To many employees, it affords interest and variety. The essential thing is for the supervisor not to place on such jobs employees who cannot easily switch from one task to another and who do their best when assigned steadily to one task until it is completed.

Role of the Employee in Planning and Scheduling

Good planning and scheduling require that the supervisor be thoroughly familiar with the work he supervises and that he have analytical ability and imagination. These are important conceptual skills. Like all of the supervisor's conceptual skills, however, they cannot be practiced separately and apart from the interpersonal aspect of supervision. Anything a supervisor does has an impact on the employees under him. If done properly, planning and scheduling can make their work easier and more satisfying. Initially, however, these operations may be disturbing to employees if they are called on to change their work habits or their working schedules.

Employees usually respond favorably to new ideas if they really understand them and if they can see some potential benefit. They, themselves, often have good ideas about the work and can invariably point out some procedural detail that the supervisor has overlooked. It is wise for a supervisor to talk freely and openly to his employees about operational problems, and he should elicit their ideas and suggestions. They will be more interested in the success of new plans and schedules if they have some part in discussing or developing them and if they believe they have contributed to a more efficient unit.

5

Delegating, Assigning, and Controlling Work

DELEGATION IS ONE OF THE MOST IMPOR-
tant and, at the same time, one of the least understood
parts of a supervisor's job. Supervisors are continually
being exhorted to delegate or to delegate more, but
rarely are they told what delegation *is* or how to do it.
This is because delegation is extremely complex and ambiguous. It is not a discrete skill in itself. Rather, it is
inextricably entwined with the conceptual skills of organizing, planning, and scheduling that have just been discussed. It is also mingled with interpersonal skills, and
it is inseparable from the personalities of the supervisor
and his subordinates. In the following example, three

different patterns of supervisory behavior in a particular situation are examined and evaluated in terms of delegation.

A supervisor was faced with a heavy workload and a deadline to meet. He had a total staff of ten technical employees, including two subordinate supervisors. While the two subordinate supervisors were responsible for different though similar aspects of the program of this unit, the heavy workload and the deadline concerned chiefly the work under subsupervisor A. The organization of the unit was as follows:

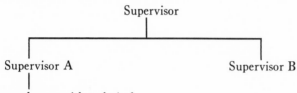

Supervisor

Supervisor A   Supervisor B

Four employees with technical
background and experience ranging
from two to five years

The supervisor had just hired two additional employees, both right out of college, and wanted to make the fullest possible use of them because of the deadline.

In the first behavior pattern, the supervisor met with the two new employees for about 15 minutes on their first day of work. He gave them a general explanation of the total program of the unit and placed particular stress on the deadline that had to be met. He gave each one an assignment to conduct research (using published sources) into one aspect of a total problem, to collect pertinent statistical data, and to write a report that interpreted the data and drew conclusions.

He told the employees that he was delegating the full responsibility for their assigned project to them. He said they were on their own because the rest of the staff was too busy to help them, but he thought they could learn more this way. He gave them several reference books and asked for a final draft of their reports one week before the deadline so he would have time to review them. Just before the interview ended, the supervisor called in one of the more senior employees, introduced him to the two new employees, told him briefly what their assignments were, and asked him to answer any questions they might have. The two new employees found out later that this senior employee was extremely busy on his own assignment, which also had a deadline, and that he was not very familiar with the particular assignment given them.

In the second behavior pattern, the supervisor (because of the heavy workload and the close deadline) believed it was essential to maintain tight control over the various segments of the project. Accordingly, he had a meeting with the two new employees and explained to them the overall program and the deadline. He gave each one reference books to read and asked them to let him know if they found anything in the books they thought could be included in the final report. If so, he would tell them what to do next. Both employees read their books but were unable to evaluate them in terms of the assigned project. They made repeated efforts to see the supervisor, but each time the supervisor's secretary said he was busy and would call the employees as soon as he was free. He never called.

In the third pattern, the day the two new employees started to work the supervisor introduced them to subsupervisor A, to whom they would be responsible. He told subsupervisor A to find something for them to do. He then left and went back to his own work and heard no more about the new employees.

The supervisor did a very poor job of delegating in all three situations. In the first behavior pattern, he undoubtedly thought he was delegating completely but he was not. He bypassed his subsupervisor A entirely. He had delegated no responsibility to subsupervisor A, who seemed to function as just another worker. We might speculate on the reasons why he was ever designated a subsupervisor.

Neither did the supervisor really delegate to the two new employees. He simply turned over an important part of his work to them, inexperienced and untested as they were. He gave them no instructions or direction, and he made no provision for their day-to-day supervision. He failed to follow up to make sure they understood what they were doing or that the project was going forward. He assigned them to a senior employee without bothering to find out how familiar the senior employee was with the particular project and without giving him any clear direction as to how he should help the new men.

This behavior was more abdication than delegation. The potentially disastrous results are obvious; a week before the deadline for completion of the project, the two new employees could hand in final drafts which might be wrong or totally inadequate.

In the second behavior pattern, the supervisor went to the opposite extreme. He would not turn over anything, either to his subsupervisor or to these two employees. The new employees could be of little value to the project. After giving them partial assignments, the supervisor failed to follow through and was unavailable to see them when they needed him. He was a bottleneck because of his insistence on doing everything himself.

The third behavior pattern was also abdication rather than delegation. This time the supervisor did not bypass his subordinate supervisor, but neither did he delegate to him. Apparently he had never discussed the hiring of these employees with the subsupervisor, nor had they jointly made any plans for the effective use of the new staff. The supervisor simply walked away from the problem. He did not follow up to see what subsupervisor A was doing in the way of training or using the new people.

The supervisor's method of delegating in each of these patterns was part and parcel of his total behavior as a supervisor. One wonders about his ability to organize the work effectively. With a total of ten subordinates, all having technical training, he hardly needed two subsupervisors. In the first two behavior patterns, he seemed to have no understanding of what the role of these subsupervisors should be or how he should use them. Subsupervisor A functioned as just another worker, and it would be interesting to know why he was made a supervisor in the first place.

Perhaps the supervisor inherited this organizational structure. It is more likely, however, that he created the two subsupervisory positions in order to pay the two men higher salaries or to reward faithful service or friendship. Whatever the reason, the organizational structure was making little contribution to the efficiency of this unit. Even in the third behavior pattern, the subsupervisor did not function in a truly supervisory capacity. He was given responsibility for finding some work for the new employees, but he apparently had no part in their selection or even in the decision to recruit two additional staff members.

The supervisor's planning and scheduling were deficient. In none of the three situations had he made any plans for integrating the new employees into the unit. In the first situation, he demonstrated a lack of judgment about his subordinates when he assigned the new employees to a senior worker who had no time to give them and who was unfamiliar with their project. The inter-action between the supervisor and his subsupervisor seemed nonexistent so far as the work was concerned, although they might have been friendly on a personal or social basis.

Process of Delegation

William H. Newman defines the process of delegation as consisting of these distinct aspects:

1. The assignment of duties by an executive to his immediate subordinates.
2. The granting of permission (authority) to make commitments, use resources, and take other ac-tions necessary to perform the duties.
3. The creation of an obligation (responsibility) on the part of each subordinate to the executive for the satisfactory performance of the duties.[1]

The assignment of duties to an immediate subordinate includes responsibility for giving clear directions to the subordinate and making sure he understands what the as-signment is and how he should carry it out. How specific the directions should be is a very important point which will be discussed later on in this chapter. The amount of permission (authority) granted to the subordinates must be commensurate with their experience and ability to use the authority wisely. In the first behavior pattern just

---

[1] William H. Newman, *Administrative Action: The Techniques of Or-ganization and Management,* Prentice-Hall, Inc., Englewood Cliffs, N.J., 1951, p. 166. Reprinted by permission of Prentice-Hall, Inc.

discussed, the supervisor gave entirely too much leeway to new, untried employees. Simply turning an employee loose is *not* delegation. The creation of an obligation (responsibility) on the part of each subordinate for the satisfactory performance of his duties requires a mechanism of follow-up and control, so that the supervisor can keep track of progress and be alert to problems.

Another important fact about delegation should be well understood. *Responsibility* cannot be delegated to others in the sense that such delegation relieves the supervisor of obligation. As was pointed out in the first chapter, *accountability* is a primary feature of supervision. A supervisor is responsible (accountable) for the work of his unit, and he cannot evade that responsibility by any amount of delegation.

The Role of Personality in Delegation

Perhaps the single most important characteristic of delegation—and the reason that good delegation is so hard to achieve—is its complexity. It is not a scientific process that can be learned. It is an integral part of the supervisor's personality makeup. And, to complicate the matter even further, it is also influenced by the subordinate.

In the case previously described, the supervisor's personality came through vividly in the first two behavior patterns. He seemed to derive a considerable amount of satisfaction from being on top of everything. In the first pattern, he seemed to be overactive; trying to handle every situation himself; becoming involved in every detail; and then bungling by his failure to organize the work, to plan ahead, to give adequate direction, or to follow through. The second behavior pattern shows much the same involvement in details, but it reveals a more cautious, restrained personality. The supervisor was afraid to let go of any part of the work, and consequently he became a bottleneck because he did not have enough time to do everything.

Both patterns show a man who would probably never be able to delegate wisely. Neither would he be able to plan, organize, or schedule work in an orderly, impersonal fashion. The personality of the subordinate supervisor was a further deterrent to effective delegation. Subsupervisor A was certainly an unassertive person; one who did not seek any delegation of authority from the supervisor. He took no initiative for the direction of his own subordinates. Instead, he was willing to wait for his supervisor to act. He probably did not want supervisory responsibility but preferred being a worker. Likewise, the senior employee whom the new men were assigned to in the first behavior pattern assumed no responsibility other than for his own work. The personalities of these two men would mesh perfectly with the need of their supervisor to be the dominant figure, handling every situation and making every decision.

Important as it is, the personality of the *subordinate* plays a secondary role in the delegation process, simply because the supervisor has superior power and influence. A supervisor normally can have the kinds of subordinates he wants. In the case just described, we can be sure that this supervisor would not have tolerated a subordinate supervisor who was very forceful or assertive.

The third behavior pattern revealed a supervisor and subsupervisor relationship that, deficient as it was, offered a great deal more hope for effective delegation. At least the supervisor's personality did not prevent him from delegating responsibility to his subsupervisor. He did delegate to him, but the process was incomplete because there was no prior consultation about hiring the new employees and no effective follow-up.

Since personality does play such an essential role in the delegation process, perhaps the first thing any supervisor should do is try to assess his own personality and the kind of subordinate response that is most satisfying. He should evaluate how he uses his own time versus the way he uses the time of his subordinates, how he perceives his subordinates, how he perceives his own superior, and how he perceives himself. To put it another way, the ability of a supervisor to delegate effectively depends on the way he relates to his job, his subordinates, his superior, and himself.

Some supervisors are incapable of delegating, no matter how much they may know about the process itself or how much they realize they should delegate. Consider two different supervisory personalities. Supervisor Green organizes his own time in such a way that he performs as much as possible of the work himself and then turns over to subordinates what he cannot do. He believes the work will not be done properly unless he does it himself. Subordinates can be assigned pieces of the work, but it is essential that he review all of it himself for accuracy and that he fit together all of the different pieces.

Mr. Green has doubts about the abilities of his subordinates to follow through on a complete project. He wants to be sure his subordinates do not get him into trouble, so he himself handles all contacts with the public, with other organizational units, or with his superior. In general, he rates his employees as average. He has the feeling that his own superior does not have a great deal of confidence in him or in his unit. He believes that his superior is watching the unit to make sure everything goes well. He thinks his superior expects him to be on top of everything that goes on. He thinks it is essential to have his hand in all details of the work, so that he will have the answers at his fingertips if his superior asks him anything. He sees himself as a careful, meticulous person who knows the work, who can be depended on, and who rarely makes mistakes.

In contrast, supervisor White believes one of his primary functions as a supervisor is to develop as fully as possible the skills, abilities, and self-confidence of his subordinates. He organizes his job so that the subordinates perform as much of the unit's work as they possibly can, thus leaving him time to think about ways to make the unit more effective. He spends a good share of his time planning future projects, working with his staff to answer questions they may have, and obtaining their ideas about the work. He expects his subordinates to assume more and more responsibility for the work as they gain experience. He believes his employees have above-average abilities and that their performance is steadily improving. Mr. White has not given too much thought to what his own superior thinks of him, but he is confident of the effectiveness of his unit, and he believes his superior is interested in overall results. If his boss asks him a question about details of the work that he does not know, he calls in the subordinate concerned and asks him to explain it to the superior. He views himself as a good leader and a person with ideas and initiative.

We can readily guess which of these two men would be more likely to delegate effectively. Supervisor Green would be very upset if he had to turn loose from the work and rely on subordinates to perform it. He does not trust them, and he lacks confidence in himself. He believes that he has continually to prove to his own superior that he is doing a good job. He would be a kind of person likely to accumulate unnecessary files and records in order to protect himself against any criticism that he failed to carry out instructions or that he made mistakes.

Mr. White, on the other hand, has a great deal of confidence in himself and his subordinates. He could very easily delegate responsibility to them. He might, in fact, be inclined to delegate too much before the employees were ready for it. Or he might have so much faith in his subordinates that he would neglect to establish adequate follow-up or controls over the work.

In these two instances we can see the effect on delegation, not only of the personalities of the supervisor and his subordinates, but also of the supervisor's relationship to his own superior. The great difference in the way these two individuals perceive their subordinates and their superiors may be partially a reflection of their own characters; but it may also reflect reality. Perhaps Mr. White's subordinates *are* much more competent and self-reliant than those of Mr. Green. Perhaps Mr. White deliberately selected employees for their initiative and abilities, whereas Mr. Green was more interested in hiring individuals who would be tractable and who would carry out his instructions faithfully and accurately. Or the difference could be accidental. Mr. Green might have taken over a unit that was already staffed with below-average employees. It is generally fair to say, however, that subordinates reflect the skill and abilities of their supervisors. A good supervisor knows how to select good employees, how to train and develop them, and how to demand superior performance from them.

These two supervisors have much less control over the behavior of their own superiors. Perhaps Mr. Green has a superior who cannot delegate, who frets about details, and who frequently intervenes in the work. Perhaps he does continually want information about all phases of Mr. Green's operations. If this is the case, a person of Mr. Green's temperament would probably be the only kind of subordinate that his superior would want. What all of this means is that one cannot delegate effectively unless he has confidence in himself and his subordinates and unless he enjoys a constructive, mature relationship with his own superior.

Vital Techniques of Delegation

William H. Newman was quoted earlier as defining delegation in terms of three aspects: (1) the assignment of duties; (2) the granting of permission or authority to take action necessary to perform the duties; and (3) the creation of an obligation or responsibility on the part of the subordinate for the satisfactory performance of the duties. We come now to the question of *how* the supervisor does these things. He does them by three vital techniques: direction, coordination, and control. We shall consider each technique separately.

Direction. Direction is, of course, the issuance of instructions to subordinates. It is the mechanism by which plans, objectives, and ideas are carried out. To a large extent, their effectiveness depends on the quality of the direction given.

Newman lists the following minimum characteristics of good instruction:

> *Compliance should be reasonable.* In thinking about whether an instruction is reasonable, an executive should

consider whether the man who will receive it has the necessary experience and ability to perform it satisfactorily. Also he should consider whether materials, equipment, external conditions, company rules, and other aspects of a total operating situation will permit the man to comply if he uses a reasonable amount of effort and ability.

The instruction should be complete. A complete order should leave no questions in the mind of the man receiving it as to what is to be done; the quality and quantity of performance that will be considered satisfactory should be understood. If it is not desired to give the man a free rein as to how the assignment is to be carried out, then the method also should be specified. And the time factor should be indicated. The quality and quantity standards combined with the time allowed for performance will, of course, have a marked effect upon whether compliance is reasonable.

The instruction is clear. The important thing is that it should be *clear to the person* receiving the order. Too often the executive giving an instruction thinks the order is clear because he has a definite picture in his own mind as to what is to be done. This is not enough. He should try to place himself in the position of the subordinate and then consider what the subordinate needs to be told. Also the language used should be readily understood by the subordinate.

Always follow up on an instruction. If an executive gives directions and then permits subordinates to decide if and when they will carry them out, the entire administration becomes lax. Time schedules lose their significance, additional inspections are necessary to discover what has and has not taken place, and the success of a subordinate depends in no small part upon his ability to guess when to take the boss seriously.[2]

[2] *Ibid.* pp. 376–378.

We can expand Newman's list by adding a very important and frequently overlooked element of good instruction—the need for a supervisor to *listen* to the employee. When giving instructions, he should obtain feedback from the employee in order to know whether the instructions have been understood. He should ask questions, and he should give the employee a chance to ask questions or to express an opinion about the instructions being given.

The employee may have very good ideas as to how the work can best be performed, what will work and what won't. After he expresses his views, it is then the supervisor's responsibility to evaluate whether the employee is right or whether he simply does not visualize the final outcome of the proposal. The supervisor must decide whether to drop the matter or whether to push ahead with it, carrying the employee along with the idea bit by bit. He should not be afraid to ask the employee, "What do you think we should do about this problem?" or "What do you suggest?" Supervisors who know how to tap the creativity and initiative of their employees enhance their own effectiveness tremendously.

Instructions may be of many different kinds, ranging from those that are highly specific and detailed to those that are so general that they more nearly resemble suggestions. Each kind of instruction has its place, depending upon circumstances and the employees involved.

New employees who are untrained in the work need specific, detailed instructions. Once they have learned the work, the kind of instruction given them need only be general. Perhaps they will need no instruction at all unless they are given a new assignment or unless the work itself changes. To continue giving an experienced, responsible employee detailed instructions is both wasteful of the supervisor's time and irritating to the employee.

Even though an employee can perform his work without additional instructions, the supervisor still needs to follow up to make sure the work is being done as planned. Very complex work or work that must meticulously follow predetermined steps and methods requires specific, detailed instructions, preferably in the form of written procedures or manuals.

Broad, general instructions are most appropriate when giving assignments to experienced employees who know the work at hand. The employees probably have ideas about the work, and they should be encouraged to initiate ways of accomplishing the assignment. General instructions, when appropriately used, can help develop initiative and resourcefulness on the part of employees.

When dealing with highly trained professional, technical, or managerial personnel, very general instructions are the rule. The supervisor should merely tell these employees what he would like done and what time limits he has in mind. The details and methods should be left to them. It would be even better if the supervisor explained the problems and discussed his overall goals with these employees and then requested them to develop plans and programs for meeting them.

Many supervisory problems result from choosing the wrong kind of instruction to use in a particular situation. A common error is overinstructing employees who are capable of working independently. At the opposite extreme are supervisors who frequently fail to give adequate direction and instruction to employees who need it, thus letting them grope and muddle through without knowing what they are doing or what is expected of them. The supervisor who turned over an important phase of a project to two brand-new employees without giving them adequate instruction or help is an example of this type of mistake. Each situation has to be judged individually. A supervisor needs to know his employees' capabilities. He should be alert to the employees' responses to his instructions and should be flexible enough to change his approach if he sees that it is not working.

Coordination. The second vital technique used in delegating is coordination. Whenever more than one employee is performing work, their various efforts have to be synchronized and meshed together so that they are all contributing to a common goal. There are various ways to achieve good coordination. One way is by organizing, planning, and scheduling the work effectively. Another way is by giving clear assignment of accountability and issuing instructions that are understood by everyone concerned. A third way is by giving the work group definite goals which each person understands and to which he is committed.

However, none of these methods can take the place of personal interaction among the supervisor and his employees and among the employees themselves. Personal interaction is the best means of assuring good coordination. Employees should be encouraged to work with each other and to coordinate their efforts. They usually will do this and will enjoy doing it if the supervisor can impart clear objectives and a sense of the importance of the project to them. Unless subordinates sincerely believe that they all are moving toward a common, important objective and that their supervisor is moving with them, the efforts of a group can be vitiated by jealousies and bickering, by jockeying for position, or by indifference. Before subordinates will function as a team, they must be convinced that their supervisor is treating each member of the group fairly and impartially, and that he recognizes the unique contributions of each one.

Control. The best instructions and the most effective

coordination can come to nothing if the supervisor does not have a means of insuring that the work is being accomplished according to plan. The control mechanism varies with different kinds of work. Some work is much easier to control than others. If it culminates in a product, a report, a program, or correspondence, the supervisor may establish control by reviewing either the completed work or a sample of the work. He may establish deadlines for completion of the project or phases of it and may require that employees keep him informed as to whether the schedule is being adhered to. He may establish checks at critical points in the work flow and may make a personal follow-up to compare expected results with actual accomplishment.

Personal follow-up with employees on the progress of the work is a very good method of control. When definite deadlines must be met, the supervisor should establish frequent check points, especially if several different employees are working on various segments of the project.

The amount and kind of control a supervisor exercises will vary with the type of work and the skill, experience, and dependability of the employees. If a supervisor has learned through experience that a subordinate always follows through on assignments and completes them on time, he will need to make only occasional checks to see how the employee is getting along. But if he has learned that an employee often forgets to do things or lets them slide, he had better follow up often and thoroughly.

Difficult-to-Control Work

A supervisor is faced with special problems when he is responsible for widely separated activities or when he has little contact with subordinates. Outside sales work is an example. It is impossible for a supervisor to know precisely what goes on during the salesman's workday. Many other types of outside work present similar problems of supervision. Routemen, telephone installers, service repairmen of all kinds, bus drivers, and policemen work with little personal contact with a supervisor. Special means of evaluation and control are necessary for these kinds of activities, since it is of prime importance that the right men be hired for the job. Reliability, initiative, and the ability to work independently are essential. A pleasant personality and high standards of conduct are equally important if the jobs involve public contact or the entering of private homes.

These men should receive training of the most intensive kind before they are left on their own. Instructions in the work and indoctrination in the applicable laws, policies, and procedures are not enough. The use of simulation or "dry runs" can be a very effective type of training for jobs that will have to deal with many different situations. A variety of test problems, resembling as nearly as possible real incidents likely to be encountered, should be posed as case studies or role-playing episodes, and the trainee should be required to deal with them. By observing the trainee's responses, the supervisor can help him overcome deficiencies and develop critical judgment and self-confidence. The supervisor should devote enough of his own time to the training of a new employee to enable him to evaluate the employee and to predict with considerable confidence whether he will succeed on the job.

Frequent follow-up is necessary once the employee is on his own. If he works in the same city as his supervisor and checks into the office each night, the supervisor should discuss with him any problems encountered during the day. Whenever possible, the employee should be given some objective standard against which his progress can be measured. Salesmen, for example, are given quotas to meet. Police officers are required to complete a report on every incident. Repairmen and installers should prepare reports or logs on the day's work. The supervisor can use these various mechanisms to judge how well the employee is doing. Some spot checking of the work by accompanying the employee on his rounds is also desirable.

When employees are scattered over a wide area, a definite means of communicating with them must be established. A supervisor should see that these employees are brought into the home office periodically for briefings or special instruction. Personal contact with the home office and with the supervisor is as important for morale purposes as it is for control. Correspondence, newsletters, and telephone communications all help to bridge the physical distance between employee and supervisor.

Some jobs that do not have the barrier of physical distance are, nevertheless, difficult to control because the supervisor cannot see or hear the employee at work. Jobs that deal with the public are of this kind. A supervisor cannot know for certain, unless he is physically present at the work site, how an employee is handling a conversation with a client. A physician cannot monitor the way his receptionist handles calls from patients because he is usually not present in the reception area. Yet the receptionist is in such a strategic spot that she can do irreparable harm to the doctor's relations with his patients and can damage his practice if she is rude and tactless or if she uses poor judgment in making appointments. Good selection and intensive training—of the simulation or "dry run" kind that has just been described— are about the only ways of insuring good performance in these cases. Furthermore, the supervisor should arrange his work in such a way that he occasionally can be present at the work site to observe the employee first hand. And he should plan to spend some time with the employee to discuss ways of handling difficult situations.

Occasionally a supervisor will use client complaints as his only control mechanism. This practice is very hazardous. In the first place, there is no assurance that clients will complain; they may just stop doing business with the offending firm. In the second place, by the time a client complains, the damage done to goodwill and client relationships may be irreparable. It is far more sensible to devise and institute positive control measures that will assure employee performance in accordance with a supervisor's policies and objectives.

6

A Further Look at Motivation

So FAR WE HAVE CONCENTRATED ON WORK and on ways a supervisor can manage it to achieve optimum results, both in terms of production and in terms of employee growth and development. We have discussed the research of Dr. Frederick Herzberg and his associates, with its emphasis on the *job* as the prime motivator and satisfier.

We have dealt primarily with the conceptual skills a supervisor should have in organizing, planning, and scheduling the work and in delegating, assigning, and controlling it. Implicit in all of this discussion has been the close interrelationship between conceptual and interpersonal skills. A supervisor cannot practice conceptual skills in a vacuum. Everything he does concerning the work has a direct effect on employees. He must take their responses into account. He must consider their feelings and attitudes, and he must find a way to integrate their goals and ambitions with his own objectives for his organization.

Supervision is indeed a complex art. This is true partly because work is complex and often hard to manage and, to an even greater extent, because the people supervised are very complex and difficult to understand. They may react in one way to a situation at one time and in an entirely different way to the same situation at another time. They may misinterpret their supervisor's efforts to help them. They may resist any change in their duties or work methods. They often show no loyalty to the supervisor or to the organization, and they do not hesitate to quit if they don't like the way things are going or if they are offered a better job somewhere else. Sometimes they act as though they do not want to work and do not want to learn.

This seemingly erratic and at times irrational behavior stems from the fact that employees do not shed their personalities, moods, and values when they come to work. Although they may present a "work face" to the supervisor, they bring with them all the fears, frustrations, hopes, ambitions, disappointments, goals, and beliefs that have shaped their personalities and their life-styles.

Tremendous amounts of time and money have been spent on efforts to learn more about how people behave, think, and feel at work; about what kind of supervision and leadership are most effective in producing the kind of employee behavior earnestly desired by every supervisor —high production, high quality, low turnover, low absenteeism, and a cheerful disposition. The research to date has resulted in greater understanding of how employees think and feel, but it has not produced any mechanism or scheme by which employees can be motivated toward goals set by a supervisor or by an organization. Much of the research is controversial, and what is accepted as truth at one time may be refuted at a later period, as additional studies reveal new truths or contradict previous findings.

It is quite possible that motivational or behavioral research will never yield specific answers or scientific tools of motivation. Most researchers observe a very limited group of employees in a limited environment responding to a limited set of conditions. It is risky to apply the conclusions derived from such a study to all employees in all environments responding to all conditions. People are not that simple. Unfortunately, sweeping generalizations have been made from limited research, and the consequences have been more harmful than beneficial. In the final analysis, each supervisor must determine his own behavior and kind of leadership in the light of his own personality and the personalities of his subordinates, the environment in which they all work, and his goals and theirs. In making this determination, it may be helpful to him to have some knowledge of the major research studies in this area and their findings.[1]

Elton Mayo and the Hawthorne Studies [2]

One of the earliest and bestknown studies was conducted by Elton Mayo and a group of associates from the Harvard Business School between 1927 and 1932; its

[1] For a readable summary of the major research on this subject, see Saul W. Gellerman, *Motivation and Productivity,* AMA, 1963.

[2] For more detail regarding Mayo's work, see Elton Mayo, *The Social Problems of an Industrial Civilization,* Harvard Business School, Boston, Mass., 1945; F. J. Roethlisberger, *Management and Morale,* Harvard University Press, Cambridge, Mass., 1939; F. J. Roethlisberger and W. J. Dickson, *Management and the Worker,* Harvard University Press, Cambridge, Mass., 1939; and Henry A. Landsberger, *Hawthorne Revisited,* Cornell University Press, Ithaca, N.Y., 1958.

focus was on the Hawthorne plant of the Western Electric Company near Chicago. The goal of this research was to find ways to increase production among groups of female assembly workers. Before Mayo and his associates were called in, company engineers had attempted to increase production by raising the level of illumination in the workrooms.

In the first series of studies, the engineers varied the level of illumination in three different departments, each doing a different kind of work and employing a different kind of worker. The results of these studies were completely erratic and inconclusive. Thinking that the results were influenced by differences in the type of work performed and by differences in the workers, the engineers conducted a second series of experiments in one department only. For this test they carefully chose two groups of operators who were comparable in age and experience. One group was placed in the test room where the engineers experimented with various levels of illumination, while the other group remained in the control room where illumination was unchanged. When they compared the production rates of the two groups they were baffled at the results, which showed that production had gone up in every room studied *including the control room,* regardless of whether the lights were brighter, dimmer, or unchanged.

The Mayo group began varying rest periods and the length of the workday in the experimental rooms; then it compared production rates with those in the control room where nothing had been changed. Special efforts were made to enlist the cooperation of the girls. The operators were chosen to participate in the study. The experiment was discussed in advance with all the employees affected, and they were asked for their assent before any of the conditions were changed.

An observer sat in the rooms to record what happened and to keep the experimental conditions steady. The researchers arrived at the same baffling results as the lighting engineers. Production soared in every room studied, including the control room, apparently without regard to the actual changes made in the length of the rest periods and the workday.

Mayo's interpretation of what happened became the basis for a "human relations" theory that has had an almost unbelievable impact on American industrial society. After sifting all the information recorded by his observers, as well as studying the logs kept by the lighting engineers, he concluded that the research team had hit upon a powerful hidden motivator. The key to increased production, he believed, was the effort of both the lighting engineers and his own research group to hold the experimental situations steady by carefully choosing operators to participate in the test and by enlisting their cooperation. In both cases, the operators became elite groups who were receiving a great deal of attention and who, for the time being, were insulated against the demands and restrictions of management.

To Mayo, the formation of a social group was the powerful stimulant to the operators. When his own researchers discussed changes with the group, asked their opinions, and permitted them to make some decisions about their working time, morale and production soared. He concluded that powerful motives could be tapped and used to improve productivity by allowing employees to form natural groups, by "treating workers like human beings," and by relieving them of impersonal control.

Mayo followed up these experiments with a massive interview program in which employees could express their feelings freely about their work. He found that employees naturally established informal groups at work and that these groups established their own production standards to which the members of the group adhered. If the groups associated themselves with management, production rose. But if they were antagonistic toward management because of impersonal treatment or excessive bossing, they restricted production to the minimum level that management would tolerate.

He concluded that the factory system, by emphasizing efficiency but failing to consider human needs, was humiliating to the human personality. It created wholesale resentment and frustration. Since most employees could not "buck" the system, they surrendered to it and became passive and inefficient producers. Mayo coined a word, *anomie,* for this employee feeling of unimportance, rootlessness, and confusion. He believed that there was a great urge on the part of workers to form groups. He thought management should take advantage of this tendency by giving groups a reasonable share of control over their own work and by showing an active, personal interest in each member of the group.

Although the Hawthorne studies were conducted between 1927 and 1932, Mayo's ideas did not catch fire until World War II. The war period created a perfect climate in which serious theories on motivation or productivity could take root. Vast war industries were being created. Thousands of workers had to be trained who had never before been in the labor force. Many of the new workers were women. Many were taken off farms and out of small towns and brought to work in war plants.

Mayo's ideas received much publicity and he, himself, promoted them with an almost evangelistic fervor. During the war period, they were embraced without reserve; "human relations" became highly fashionable. During the

1940's and early 1950's, the idea prevailed that the paramount goal of management should be to keep employees happy. If employee happiness were maintained, everything else would follow—production and quality would be high, employees would work hard, and they would strive to improve and to learn. However, if employee happiness were interfered with, all would be lost. The whole structure of productivity and plant efficiency would collapse. The principal job of supervisors was seen as one of keeping employees free from stress and of encouraging social groups at work.

Thousands of plant foremen and supervisors were run through canned training programs in job relations, one of the courses in the famous wartime "training within industry" series. Although old-time supervisors never really accepted the human relations ideas, they tried to conform and to adjust their supervisory practices to fit the new mold. Individuals who became supervisors for the first time in those years tended to function as a combination of social director and father confessor to their employees. Discipline became lax. Rest periods and coffee breaks were introduced, counselors were hired to discuss employees' personal problems with them, and industry spent vast sums of money on employee recreational and social activities.

The human relations school suffered a severe jolt from the two recessions of the 1950's. Seeing profits drop and competition intensify, management asked itself if keeping employees happy really did result in high production. The answer was no. When it began to take stock of what had happened during the human relations era, management found that production had been declining, sloppy or defective work had been tolerated, and supervisors did not dare discipline employees or require a high standard of performance. Overpermissiveness was the order of the day.

The human relations era began to draw to a close, not only because of the changed attitude of management, but also because further research had begun to cast doubt on the interpretations and conclusions derived from the Hawthorne studies. Since that time, Mayo's theories have been accepted more for their historical contribution to behavioral science than as a guide for action.

There is little doubt that Mayo hit upon some major truths regarding the industrial environment and the attitudes of industrial workers. The destructive effects of the plant assembly line on employee interest and initiative are now generally acknowledged. Mayo may have inferred too much about the urge of employees to form social groups at work, but his observation that employee groups set and maintain their own production standards has much validity.

The major weakness in Mayo's theory is the sweeping generalization derived from his observations, which took place in a very limited setting. This particular group of employees no doubt did respond to the increased attention given them by producing at a higher rate. The question is whether they would indeed have *continued* to produce at a higher rate if personal attention and consideration had become a permanent way of life in the plant. We would expect a similar burst of production from any group of employees who were doing routine, boring work and who were accustomed to being ignored and treated as machines if, all of a sudden, they received a great deal of attention and implicit approval from management. The contrast between their new status and their ordinary, humdrum working conditions could account for increased production and increased morale. However, we could also expect that these positive effects would be temporary and would soon wear off once the employees became accustomed to their new environment. A perpetual state of euphoria is very hard to maintain. Even if it were maintained, it would probably not be very conducive to initiative and creativity. It is also doubtful that other kinds of employees such as highly skilled technicians, professional people, or managers would have responded in similar vein to the experimental atmosphere created by the researchers.

Another weakness in the conclusions drawn from the Hawthorne studies is their failure to consider the need for an exceptional kind of supervisor in order to make the theory work. Thousands of supervisors were exhorted to treat employees as human beings. They tried to apply a canned approach to human relations. But what was really needed was a new kind of imaginative supervisor who could continually find *new* ways to challenge and interest his employees. This, of course, would have been a very big order for any supervisor to fill.

Finally, the theory failed because it smacked of manipulation. Many managers and supervisors did not sincerely believe in the idea of employee participation in decision making. Therefore, they tried to make employees feel they were participating; in fact, the supervisors were keeping a tight rein on all decisions. Employees saw through this hypocrisy and resented it.

Production-Centered Versus Employee-Centered Supervision

A series of studies conducted by the University of Michigan attempted to observe the effect of supervisory behavior on worker productivity.[3] The first of the studies, by Rensis Likert and Daniel Katz, was conducted on a clerical group in an insurance company. By means of patterned interviews, the researchers found two major categories of supervisors: those who were *production-centered* and those who were *employee-centered*.

A production-centered supervisor considered his main job to be getting the work done. He thought of his employees primarily as instruments for doing this, rather than as human beings with needs and emotions. He did not hesitate to step into the work whenever he saw something being done that he did not like. He handled some of the work personally when he thought that was the best way of completing it. He gave specific instructions and made sure they were followed. He was far more active and driving than the employee-centered supervisor.

An employee-centered supervisor, on the other hand, considered supervision rather than production to be his main job. He gave his employees a general outline of how the work was to be accomplished and left the details to them. He did not check closely to be sure the work was done; rather he believed his employees were responsible enough to get the work done without the need for his checking.

After identifying the two kinds of supervisors, the researchers studied the production records of the units under each type. They concluded that employee-centered

[3] See Daniel Katz et al., *Productivity, Supervision and Morale in an Office Situation,* University of Michigan Institute for Social Research, Ann Arbor, Mich., 1950; Rensis Likert, "Measuring Organizational Performance," *Harvard Business Review,* March–April 1958; Victor H. Vroom and Floyd C. Mann, "Leader Authoritarianism and Employee Attitudes," *Personnel Psychology,* Summer 1960; and Victor H. Vroom, *Some Personality Determinants of the Effects of Participation,* Prentice-Hall, Inc., Englewood Cliffs, N.J., 1960.

supervisors were likely to be in charge of high producing groups and that production-centered supervisors were likely to be in charge of low producing groups. They interpreted this finding to mean that employee-centered supervision *resulted* in higher production.

These conclusions have provoked much controversy. They have been criticized for confusing cause and effect. The employee-centered supervisors might have been able to perform the way they they did *because* they happened to have mature and effective groups, while the production-centered supervisors had no choice in the way they acted because of the inefficiency of their groups. Indeed, it would seem that a serious omission in the study was the failure to evaluate the employees in the different groups.

A subsequent study contradicted somewhat the conclusions that employee-centered supervision *always* leads to higher production. Researchers selected four approximately equal clerical divisions all doing the same kind of work. They placed two of the groups under a production-centered supervisor and the other two under an employee-centered supervisor. After a year, the groups under the production-centered supervisor had achieved a 25 percent increase in productivity, while the increase in productivity of the groups under the employee-centered supervisor was 20 percent.

Victor H. Vroom and Floyd C. Mann conducted another study in a large trucking company. They observed two different groups, package handlers and truck drivers, and their dispatchers. The package handlers worked in small, closely knit units. The nature of their work required considerable teamwork and more or less constant contacts between the men and their supervisor. They showed a preference for employee-centered supervisors.

The truck drivers and their dispatchers spent the major part of their time alone or out of contact with each other. Getting the work done was a highly individual matter to them and they scarcely depended on each other at all, except that the truck drivers required accurate information from the dispatchers. These employees favored authoritarian or production-centered supervisors.

Vroom and Mann concluded that the *nature of the job* determined the most effective kind of supervision. In jobs requiring considerable teamwork, the main danger to morale and productivity is dissension, and a democratic supervisor who supports the workers' egos and keeps things on an even keel is most effective. Where work is more an individual matter, the essential ingredient is not harmony but confidence that one knows what is expected of him. In this situation, an authoritarian supervisor with a firm, no-nonsense attitude is more effective.

Vroom has also found in other studies that the effects of supervision may depend to a considerable extent on the *personality of the individual worker*. If a man has strong qualities of independence and is not particularly awed by people who hold positions of authority, he prefers to have a say in decisions affecting his work. He will be more productive under a participative (employee-centered) supervisor. However, there are many people who are more dependent and who prefer to carry out the orders of a strong leader rather than decide for themselves what to do.

Vroom's observations make a great deal of sense. Of course, there is a danger in carrying either of these two kinds of supervision too far. The right balance has to be maintained, and the supervisor's approach should be modified to suit individual situations.

Theory X and Theory Y

The late Douglas McGregor of the Massachusetts Institute of Technology believed that the way men managed or supervised reflected their basic philosophies and attitudes toward people. He defined two distinct philosophies of management, which he called Theory X and Theory Y.[4]

Theory X is authoritarian. It assumes that most people do not like to work, that some kind of club has to be held over their heads to make them work, and that most people would rather be told what to do than think for themselves. McGregor believed that these assumptions about people were the basis for the classical theories of organization with their emphasis on centralized authority and control.

Theory Y assumes that people do not inherently dislike work but that they develop attitudes toward work based on their experiences with it. While authoritarian methods can get things done, they are not the only methods for doing so. People will select goals for themselves if they see the possibility of some kind of reward, either monetary or in the form of personal satisfaction. Once they have selected a goal, they will pursue it as vigorously as they would if their superiors were trying to pressure them into doing the same thing. Under the right circumstances, people do not shun responsibility but seek it. McGregor believed the task of management under Theory Y was to make the job the principal stage on which the enlargement of competence, self-control, and a sense of accomplishment could occur.

[4] Douglas McGregor, *The Human Side of Enterprise,* McGraw-Hill Book Company, New York, 1960.

The latter observation coincides with the behavioral scientists' theories of organization, with their emphasis on more fluid jobs and less structure and organizational controls. It also comes very close to the views of Frederick Herzberg that the *job* is the real motivator.

The Managerial Grid

Robert Blake and Jane Mouton have depicted five different theories of managerial and supervisory behavior along a grid using two variables, *concern for people* and *concern for production*.[5] (See Exhibit 7.)

The style *1.1* represents minimal concern for production and minimal concern for people. This is the passive, laissez-faire style of supervision. Style *1.9* at the top left corner represents maximal concern for people and minimal concern for production. This style reflects the human relations school of thought; that is, that the primary job of the supervisor is to keep employees happy and free from stress and, if this is done, high production will automatically follow.

The *9.1* style in the lower right corner shows maximal concern for production and minimal concern for people. This style represents authoritarian supervision. The supervisor makes all decisions and passes them down to employees in the form of orders and directives. The *9.9* style in the upper right corner shows maximal concern for both production and people. This is the ideal form of leadership, in the view of Blake and Mouton.

The *5.5* style in the middle of the grid attempts to

[5] *The Managerial Grid,* Gulf Publishing Co., Houston, Tex., 1964.

Exhibit 7

THE MANAGERIAL GRID

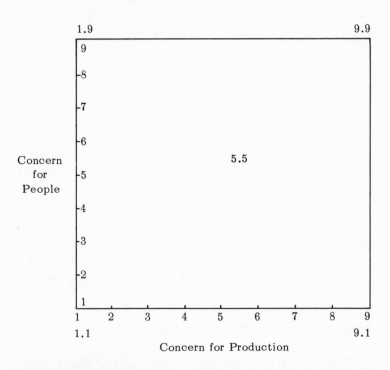

compromise concern for production and concern for people. This is the style of the middle-of-the-road supervisor who would probably try to suppress or compromise conflicts rather than bring them out into the open and attempt to solve them. He would try to negotiate differences or trade off conflicting views and goals. The ideal 9.9 supervisor, on the other hand, develops committed people sharing common goals. Conflicts are squarely faced and resolved in an atmosphere of openness and trust.

Individual Motivation

Now that we have summarized briefly a few of the studies in employee motivation and behavior, we should try to put them into perspective. It was noted that all of the research involved limited groups of employees in limited settings. Moreover, the researchers began their investigations with hypotheses that were narrowly defined. None of the studies attempted to produce a general theory of motivation that would apply to all people in every circumstance. For these reasons, it is very dangerous to deduce too much from any of the research. The greatest contribution the studies have made has been in the thought they have provoked about the various elements in the work situation and the influence these elements have on employee productivity, morale, and creativity.

Motivation is very complex and is inseparable from an individual's life goals, his values and psychic needs, and his life experiences. What motivates one employee or group of employees may fail completely to motivate another. The entrepreneur who risks his life savings to start a business certainly does not have the same motivation as a bookkeeper who works in the same job for the same firm for 30 years. A woman clerical employee who works to help support and educate a growing family does not have the same relish for job challenge and responsibility as an ambitious young man right out of college who is embarked on a business career.

The same individual may have entirely different motivation at different times of his life. For example, a man with a family to support may have been out of work for some time. The only thing that motivates him at this time is the need for security. If he finds a job with steady work and pay, the regularity of his pay check will be sufficient motivation *for a while*. He will not be too concerned about job challenge, or the opportunity to grow and develop, or the kind of supervision he receives. However, after he has been on the job long enough for his financial pressure to have eased, he and his family will begin to relax. Then the regularity of the pay check will cease being enough. He and his wife might have a strong desire for a more active social life, and he might be motivated by the opportunity for increased socialization through his work. He and his family might make new friends among his co-workers, or they might participate in organized company recreational activities such as bowling leagues or bridge clubs. This motivation also will have a finite life span.

Once the needs for security and socialization have been satisfied, he will acquire other needs. He may begin to feel that his work is dull and monotonous, that he has the ability to handle much more responsibility, and that his supervisor does not recognize his capabilities or give him enough credit for what he does. The desire for esteem may become his prime motivator. Depending upon his personality, he may be satisfied temporarily with some form of award or election to union shop steward. If he is ambitious, he may aspire to become a supervisor. Abraham Maslow has termed these ascending motivators as the "hierarchy of need," and he has identified them as security, social, esteem, autonomy, and self-actualization.[6] Before a higher need can be satisfied, a lower one must be met. Conversely, once a lower need has been satisfied, most individuals move on to a higher one.

Needs of individuals may begin at different points in this ascending scale. Many young college graduates today

[6] "A Theory of Human Motivation," *Psychological Review*, Vol. 50, 1943.

have been raised during a period of economic ease and are not concerned with security. They are not motivated to the extent that their parents might have been by a steady, secure job. Their social needs may have been fulfilled in college and elsewhere. The chief motivators for them may be the needs at higher points in the scale, such as esteem, autonomy, and self-actualization.

Many of today's young people also are motivated by the need to serve humanity or to make a contribution to society. This may be a part of self-actualization on Maslow's scale. It serves as such a powerful motivator in some individuals that it may be a separate need altogether.

Many people are strongly motivated by the desire to be needed or the desire to help other people. It is usually assumed that one of the principal reasons young women go into such fields as nursing is their strong desire to be needed and to help people. The same need may dominate a person's life outside of work. For example, it may induce a woman to marry a man who is weak in character and personality and who is somewhat deficient at making a living.

The need to be needed can drive people to tremendous accomplishment at work if they are in circumstances where this need can be met. A housewife went to work to supplement the family income and to help educate her children. Economic considerations were one force that induced her to work. Another equally powerful one was the need to be needed, both by her family in the form of the additional income she could provide and by her employer. She started work as a bookkeeper for a small businessman who had just opened his business and was struggling to make a go of it. She soon became a driving force that helped propel him to success. She poured herself into the work. She assiduously collected his accounts; at the same time she established excellent relations with his customers and also with his creditors. She watched expenditures like a hawk and was able to curb the owner's profligate tendencies with both his personal and his business funds. She was grossly underpaid and unappreciated. The owner had very little understanding of the contribution she was making and no recognition of the drives that were compelling her to make the contribution. After 20 years of her firm control over the purse strings, the company had expanded enormously and the owner had become wealthy. His bookkeeper never shared in the material rewards. She did, however, derive great satisfaction from seeing the contribution she had made to the success of the business.

Life experiences can have a tremendous influence on a person's motivation, but the same experiences can have an entirely different effect on someone else. One individual whose parents ignored him during his childhood or adolescence or who downgraded his abilities and accomplishments may develop a powerful drive to succeed and to prove himself. This drive may push him forward throughout his life. Another person with the same experience may accept the lower evaluation of himself given by others and avoid challenge for fear of failure. He may settle for a humdrum life with security.

An individual who starts his career with drive and ambition may lose them through a series of failures and rebuffs. He may accept a passive, cautious role and stop trying to achieve. The same failures and rebuffs may give another person an even greater determination to succeed.

Most people modify their self-evaluations as they go through life. Some continually set higher goals and challenges for themselves, while others restrict their ambitions and goals. A person who has lost his motivation and self-confidence through a series of misfortunes may regain them if he has a chance to taste success. Such a person would be fortunate to work for a supervisor who is sensitive and alert enough to see the potential beneath his protective coat of caution and pessimism and who will give him the support and encouragement he needs for success.

Motivating Power of Money

How strong and durable is pay as a motivator? Herzberg calls it a "hygienic factor," which does not motivate but merely sustains motivation in the sense that inadequate pay may cause a person to lose motivation or to become dissatisfied.

Pay can serve as a powerful motivator when it is directly tied to performance or accomplishment. Even here, however, its role is difficult to measure. We can conclude from observation that a salesperson who is paid a commission usually works much harder at selling than does a salesperson who is paid a straight salary. Bonuses that are given for specific accomplishments or for a specific performance are certainly motivators. Many executive compensation plans base salaries, to an extent, on an increase in the company's sales or earnings. Money undoubtedly has a motivating influence in these cases. Piece rates or incentive systems based on specific output probably have a motivating effect. We cannot be entirely sure of this, however, because of the psychological factors and group pressures that often operate to hold down the output of the fastest employees or the rate busters. If an employee has worked particularly hard and has done an unusually good job and then is immediately given a raise in recognition of his accomplishment, the money serves to motivate him to continued effort. But it is often easier to see the relationship between damage to motivation or morale caused by inadequate pay or the withholding of a pay raise or promotion when it has been earned.

More often than not, pay has no direct relationship to performance. Under civil service systems and most union contracts, pay increases are granted automatically on the basis of length of service. The pay scale itself is supposed to be related to the difficulty of the work performed, but this relationship is frequently breached because of the lack of enforcement of job evaluation standards. Automatic pay increases or promotions have virtually no motivational value. If an employee knows that his salary and his status will increase even if he turns in a minimal performance, the expected increase will not serve as a motivator for improved performance.

Humans are insatiable in their desires and needs, both economic and psychic. As soon as one need is satisfied, another one takes its place. So it is with money. A pay raise serves only as a temporary satisfier. If an employee feels that he is underpaid, a raise will overcome those feelings for the time being. But he will become dissatisfied again unless his salary is continually raised. There is no possible way that money can make a person happy permanently. This fact either is unknown or is overlooked by many supervisors who believe that all personnel problems can be solved by granting a pay raise or a promotion. This is a short-sighted approach. Even worse, it does not work. A supervisor cannot keep employees happy with money alone. There must be other, more enduring satisfactions in the job.

There also can be undesirable psychological effects of raising employees' salaries too often and too much or of promoting employees too rapidly. If their job responsibilities and their contributions to the organization do not keep pace with their salary increases, the employees may develop a blasé attitude about pay and simply take higher and higher salaries for granted. Or they may become concerned with nothing but money and continually press for more. Or they may become very unhappy with their job assignments. They may reason, "Anybody getting as high a salary as I am ought to have a lot more status and authority than I have around here."

Too many pay raises too fast or too many promotions can make an employee feel guilty about how little he actually is contributing for the pay he is receiving. His guilt may result in poor performance or in such undesirable behavior as excessive drinking. Individuals who have very low self-esteem may feel very guilty if they believe they are overpaid. Paying these employees slightly *less* than they are worth may result in the most satisfaction for them.

There is another aspect to money as a motivator that is often overlooked. An employee's salary is not an absolute quantity. It is relative. He views his salary in relation to that of his co-workers or his associates outside of work. It is these comparisons that usually cause employees to become dissatisfied with their pay. If an employee believes that his salary is too low in relation to what is paid other employees doing comparable work, or work having comparable responsibility, he will be dissatisfied. It is the inequity of the situation that rankles him more than the absolute dollars and cents. Furthermore, if all his friends outside of work are earning more money than he is, he may become dissatisfied with his pay and also with his job.

Pay administration is not an easy chore, and the relationship between pay and motivation is often very obscure. Supervisors, of course, should see that employees under their supervision are treated equitably and that they are recognized and rewarded for superior achievement. By keeping open the channels of communication with his employees, a supervisor can usually detect dissatisfaction over pay or other working conditions and can clarify misunderstandings before they become serious.

Role of Negative Incentives

The behavioral science literature stresses almost exclusively positive motivational factors; that is, those forces that make an employee want to do his best or to achieve. Negative factors can also be very powerful, and both positive and negative factors should be used. Earlier we cited the case of a man who had just found a job after being unemployed for some time. He was strongly motivated by a desire for security. Fear of being fired (a distinctly negative incentive) was the most powerful motivator possible for him at that time. That fear controlled his punctuality, his attendance, and his performance more than anything else could have. If the man had worked under a lax supervisor, however, and if he had soon found that he could do almost anything he wanted without being fired, this incentive could have lost its power and his performance, attendance, and punctuality might have deteriorated.

Most employees have a latent fear of being fired and a desire to avoid the displeasure or criticism of the boss. These are strong motivators as long as the supervisor maintains discipline and demands a high standard of performance. A desire to avoid conflict with co-workers may also be a powerful incentive for cooperation.

Danger in Oversimplifying Motivation

The foregoing discussion should have made clear the complexity and difficulty—and also the instability—of human motivation. Trained psychologists have been unable to assess or measure it accurately or even to comprehend its dimensions. Supervisors should be very wary of trying to analyze the motivation of individual employees. It is doubtful that any supervisor really knows enough about an employee or the employee's life experiences to know what motivates him.

Great harm can result from off-the-cuff diagnoses by supervisors. It is very easy to oversimplify what seem to be reasons for an employee's actions. It is very easy to jump to conclusions or to place people in motivational categories on the basis of flimsy evidence. The case we mentioned earlier of a man who had lost his drive and ambition because of traumatic experiences would have deceived a good number of supervisors. Based on their observation of the man's behavior, they would have concluded that security was his strongest motivator, and consequently they would have assigned him to a routine job with clearly defined duties and little challenge. Because of their assumptions and oversimplifications, they might have missed a striking opportunity to help an employee and perhaps unleash a driving force that could have contributed much to their organizations.

Many supervisors erroneously assume that women employees have less drive for achievement than men because they have had experience with *some* women employees who did not want challenge or responsibility.

Supervisors may confuse drive and motivation with bombast and may completely overlook the strong motivation of employees who go about their work quietly. The chances of error are great in any amateur analysis of this complex part of human personality.

Nevertheless, a knowledge of some of the motivating forces can increase a supervisor's understanding of his employees and of the reasons why they react as they do. No theory can be an effective substitute for his close interpersonal relations with them. By talking to them and working with them, by listening to what they say and don't say, and partly by trial and error, he can learn what kind of job climate and what kind of supervisory behavior will bring out the best in them.

7

$\mathcal{M}$aintaining High $\mathcal{P}$erformance

$\mathcal{A}$s WAS SAID IN THE PRECEDING CHAPTER,
the supervisor should not assume the role of amateur
psychologist in trying to analyze the motives of his employees. The chance of error is great and the consequences can be quite harmful. A supervisor's attitudes
and actions toward an employee may be strongly influenced by his diagnosis of the employee's motives. If the
diagnosis is wrong, the employee will respond negatively
and not perform in the way the supervisor expects him
to. Yet the supervisor may be so sure that his own evaluation is right that he will continually miss opportunities
to reach the employee or to stimulate and develop him.

Our motives and innermost thoughts usually are well
hidden. Sometimes we deliberately conceal them and talk
and act in such a way that the observer will be thrown off

the track and will ascribe totally spurious motives to us. It is fortunate that the human mind and personality are so abstruse. If our thoughts and motives were readily apparent, anyone with a little training in psychology could manipulate and control us.

Supervisors have a great deal of power over employees. To a large extent the employee's career, his development and advancement, and even his station in life are dependent upon his supervisor. He would be very vulnerable to an unscrupulous supervisor if his thoughts and motives could be easily read. Some supervisors do try to manipulate employees on the basis of what they believe to be the employees' vulnerable spots. In a free society, however, employees are not helpless. In a highly industrialized society, they have considerable power—both through unions and as individuals—because of the market demand for trained workers. Furthermore, the supervisor may not be the only one who knows something about human motivation. The employee may know just as much. Perhaps he has analyzed his supervisor's motives and is trying to manipulate *him*. We then have a mutual manipulation, probably with both sides missing the target so far as sizing up the other is concerned.

A healthier state of affairs is a mutual respect and understanding between supervisor and employee. The most successful supervisors have an inherent warmth, a sincere interest in seeing that employees develop, and a sensitivity to the feelings and needs of others. They are usually able to establish rapport with the employee so that communication between them remains free and open.

A supervisor need not continually be *doing* something in order to maintain high performance and morale. The tone and climate he establishes, the standards he maintains, the example he sets, the kind of performance he requires, and the reward system he uses have tremendous impact on both performance and morale. A very successful football coach was hired to manage a chronically losing team, and his first public statement was, "I will demand excellence." Demanding excellence and inspiring employees to believe that they are *capable* of excellence are often the best ways of obtaining it.

Supervisors generally have three categories of employees: (1) those who are above average, (2) those who perform acceptably, and (3) those whose performance is unsatisfactory.

The Above-Average Employee

Contrary to general belief, the above-average employee may present the supervisor with his greatest challenge. This employee's performance should not be taken for granted, although supervisors sometimes do just that. It is necessary to sustain the employee's motivation, high performance, and interest. This means that the supervisor must assess the special abilities and aptitudes of the employee and must determine the approach most likely to increase his value and development. The best way to make this assessment is to place the employee in different test situations and observe his responses.

A supervisor may use test situations that already exist in the employee's job merely by giving him more independence and more responsibility, or giving him less specific instructions, or leaving him more initiative for starting and following up on tasks. Or the supervisor may temporarily assign the employee other work that affords more challenge and is more difficult. Any work given to the employee other than his regular job should not be so ambitious or so urgent that the employee could not be taken off it if necessary without harming the project. Before an employee is taken off his regular job and assigned to some other work, the supervisor should carefully discuss his plans with the employee and should be sure he understands the reason for the assignment and wants to try it. The employee may not be interested in any other assignment besides his regular job.

By giving the employee different degrees of responsibility and increasingly difficult tasks and observing the way he handles them, the supervisor should be able to obtain answers to the following questions: Is the employee happiest and most productive when he is given more challenging work or when he is given greater independence to carry it out? Does he respond well to an assignment given him in broad, general terms so that he will have to figure out how to do it, or does he become upset and confused in these situations? Does he perform best those everyday duties that he knows thoroughly? Is he more productive and happier when he feels free to call upon the supervisor for help and when he is sure of the limits to his authority? The employee might also be given test assignments that require him to deal with people. Situations could range in difficulty from giving out information that is fairly routine to negotiating an agreement in a difficult case.

The supervisor can use the knowledge thus acquired to plan ways of developing the employee. He should recognize that some people are most productive when their assignments are open-ended and when they have to make many decisions themselves. Others do their best work in jobs that are structured, when they know exactly what they are supposed to do, and when the supervisor is available to help them. These employees may just want to be left alone and not pushed to assume more responsibility. Both kinds of employees may be above average. Some employees are very good at working with people, but others are not and prefer jobs without a great deal of interpersonal contact. Not everyone craves challenge and responsibility. Those who do will soon become unhappy if their jobs do not provide these, but those who dislike a lot of responsibility for independent action and decision will become anxious and unsure of themselves if they are forced to accept it.

The supervisor should be aware of these differences. Based on observed facts, he should be able to make an objective evaluation of the kind of work an individual employee is best suited for. Then he should make every effort to give the employee the type of assignment for which he is suited and which will afford him the best opportunity for development.

Employees with high potential should not be pushed into incompatible jobs in order to give them a higher salary or a promotion. An employee whose performance has been above average may turn into a poor performer on the wrong kind of job. Poor placement can create much damage to the employee and to the organization. Often the damage is insidious because it does not show up for months or years.

Poor placement can occur at any level of an organization. Many middle- and senior-level employees are promoted into jobs for which they are unsuited. For example, employees who have spent years doing research in a narrow field may be promoted to administrative jobs or jobs that require the coordination of multiple operations. Introverts who have spent years working alone may be promoted to jobs supervising large groups of employees.

A supervisor should not try to push an above-average

employee who is perfectly happy doing his present job and just wants to be left alone. As time goes on, the employee may want to take on more responsibility, especially if he sees it as the only way to get a promotion. But he may have already decided that he prefers job satisfaction to more money. He may want to forgo substantial monetary rewards with the headaches and ulcers that go with them and accept a comfortable, stress-free job that satisfies him even though it commands a lower salary.

One of the ways, then, that a supervisor can maintain the high performance of above-average employees is to assess their abilities and interests by objective means and try to give them assignments for which they are best suited, providing challenge and responsibility for those who want and will accept it.

Need for Recognition

Another way of maintaining high performance is by giving the employee adequate and timely recognition. Here we must return briefly to the subject of pay. As was noted in the previous chapter, pay is most powerful as an incentive when it is tied directly to performance. The employee who is doing a truly superior job should receive a pay raise, or he should be promoted to a higher level if his duties and responsibilities warrant it.

Employees are concerned about the relationship of their salaries to those of other employees. If they believe they are performing work superior in quality to or greater in difficulty than that performed by their co-workers who are receiving equal or higher salaries, they are likely to become discouraged or to lose interest. One of the major weaknesses in most civil service pay plans is that they do not distinguish between the employee who is barely acceptable and the one who is performing in an excellent fashion. It is also a weakness in many occupations covered by union agreements. All employees receive the union scale, and supervisors are wary of paying individual employees premium rates above the scale for fear they will establish a precedent or set the stage for a demand by the union for a higher minimum scale for everyone. As illustrated by the following example, an egalitarian policy can be demoralizing to the superior employee.

Two butchers had been working for years in the meat department of a large supermarket. They were skilled and fast at their trade. They also were pleasant and obliging, and over the years they had built up a very large clientele of regular customers who always asked for them. The manager of the meat department paid them the union scale, which was what he paid all of his other butchers including those who were new and several who worked only one or two days a week. The two butchers asked him several times for a raise. He repeatedly told them he would try to do something about it, but nothing ever happened and the men finally quit. They went to work for another market, taking many of their regular customers with them. It was possible they received the same treatment from their new employer, but at least they had the human satisfaction of striking a blow at the boss.

If there are particular reasons why an employee who is doing a superior job cannot be promoted or given a raise, the supervisor has an obligation to discuss the matter with the employee and let him know the reasons. At the same time, he should show the employee that he does appreciate his contribution. He should not ignore the employee's accomplishments or attempt to downgrade them as an excuse for not granting the raise. Supervisors sometimes evade the problem by leading an employee to believe that a raise will be forthcoming and then doing nothing about it. This results in increased resentment on the part of the employee.

Judgment should be used in granting pay raises. We have been discussing one common problem, where employees doing an exceptional job feel they are not being recognized. Some supervisors make the opposite mistake and go overboard in raising an employee whom they consider to be good or to have potential or whom they like. They may give the employee repeated raises or promotions before his contribution has justified them or before his knowledge and skill have increased enough to keep pace with his salary.

There are several undesirable effects of a too-liberal policy of raises or promotions. For one thing, there is always a ceiling to raises; pay cannot be increased indefinitely. In a short time the employee will have reached his ceiling. The raises will cease and he will begin to get dissatisfied. He may associate the increases with his personal worth, his personality, or his friendship with his supervisor rather than with his contribution, since there has been little connection between the two. When the raises stop, he may believe he has been rejected or abandoned by his supervisor.

Another result is that the employee is likely to acquire an overinflated opinion of himself and his value to the organization, and he may not apply himself as diligently as he should. His attitude may retard his growth and development. Or he may become cocky and arrogant and have trouble in working with other people throughout the organization.

Finally, supervisors have been known to change their minds about an employee's worth. After promoting a person rapidly, the supervisor may, upon closer observation, decide that the employee does not have the ability or the potential which had been assumed and that his performance is not justifying the salary he is receiving.

Performance Awards

Some organizations use various kinds of performance awards as a way of recognizing employees' superior attainments, especially in situations where pay raises cannot be given. Such awards have an effect similar to that of pay increases. They may be a success or a failure as incentives, depending upon the way they are used. Just as scarce commodities command a higher price, performance awards have a higher value when they are made scarce. They should be given only for achievement that is genuinely noteworthy. Awards are effective only if they have credibility in the eyes of employees. The employees must believe that those who receive them have really earned them. If awards become commonplace or if employees think they are given to individuals who are usually the supervisor's pets, they will have no value. In fact they may be detrimental, causing dissatisfaction on the part of employees who fail to receive them.

Average Employees

Every supervisor has some employees who do an acceptable job but no more. What should he do about these employees? Should he try to improve their performance, or should he leave them alone? There is no clear-cut answer, for the supervisor needs to determine why the employees are performing no better than they are.

If the employee is interested and seems to be doing his very best, it may be difficult for the supervisor to improve his performance. The employee may be doing as well as his mental abilities permit. On the other hand, training in some specific aspect of the work may improve performance. He may be deficient in some skill or may have insufficient technical background for the work. Clerical employees may perform at a barely acceptable level because they are deficient in typing skill or in grammar, spelling, or some other subject. Intensive training in these subjects may markedly improve the employee's performance. If such training is not available within the company or organization, the local public schools generally have evening classes in all of these subjects. The employee should be encouraged to take such training. If his performance is marginal, he may be required to take the training as a condition of continued employment.

Employees in professional or technical fields very often do not have the knowledge and professional skill that they are presumed to have. The supervisor should make a critical evaluation of the employee's professional background and should make sure that he obtains further training to counter his deficiencies.

An employee may not be interested in the work. He may not understand how or why it is being done. He may not be sure what he is supposed to do. Also, an employee may be poor at certain duties. Some people are utterly incapable of handling details. They forget to do things; they keep inaccurate records; they make repeated clerical mistakes. These employees can be very exasperating if they are in jobs where details are important. If the supervisor is convinced that the deficiencies are a part of the employee's makeup and that he cannot or will not correct them, he should not retain the employee in that job. For example, some employees are lost when it comes to working with numbers. They should not be hired (or retained) as bookkeepers or accountants or statistical clerks. The supervisor should try to determine whether an employee has the necessary aptitude and skill for a particular job. He might experiment with a change in duties or assignment to see if the employee's performance improves.

There are some people who simply do not have the drive, the initiative, the energy, or the interest to do more than average work. These employees do what they are told and carry out the assignments given them, but they do not initiate things or follow through without being pushed. Their supervisors have to follow up continually to make sure things have been done. Often this kind of behavior is part of the employee's personality, or it may be part of his physiology. He may be lazy or he may be more interested in things outside of work. This type of employee is one of the most difficult to motivate. He is usually pleasant and agreeable and easy to get along with. There may be no way for a supervisor to improve his performance. If he is retained at all, he should be placed in a routine job where his lethargy and lack of drive may be of less consequence.

The Unsatisfactory Employee

There are employees who try the souls of supervisors. They often consume an enormous amount of the supervisor's time. Usually they are unproductive and represent a heavy cost to the organization. Sometimes they are long-service employees who have a vested interest in their jobs because of their seniority. Supervisors frequently try to work around them, in effect pushing them to the side while hiring additional employees to get the work done. This approach, of course, evades the problem and often aggravates it. An effective supervisor is not content to have any unsatisfactory employees on his staff. In general, he has three ways of dealing with them: (1) He can try to improve the employee's performance; (2) he can have the employee transferred to another job or to another unit; and (3) he can discharge the employee. Each course of action has its value in particular circumstances.

Often there is no clear-cut distinction between the average employee and the unsatisfactory employee. The difference may be only a matter of degree. If an average employee performs at a barely acceptable level, or if he requires an excessive amount of supervision and follow-up, he might be classed as unsatisfactory for all practical purposes.

The best approach for a supervisor to take in dealing with unsatisfactory performance will depend upon several factors. Foremost is the question of how long an employee has been unsatisfactory. Is he a new employee or one with long service? If he is a long-service employee, has his performance been unsatisfactory for years or has there been a marked decline recently?

A second important question is in what respect the employee's performance is unsatisfactory. Is he frequently tardy or absent from work? Is the quantity and quality of his work unacceptable? Does he have constant friction with his co-workers or his supervisor? In some cases, an employee may be deficient in all of these respects.

The third question that should be considered is what

the causes of the unsatisfactory performance are. Many different things influence job performance. The employee's own ability and personality, factors within the job or its environment, and pressures outside of work all have a bearing. To a considerable degree, successful management of poor performance depends upon the accuracy of the supervisor's evaluation of the nature and cause of the deficiency.

Poor Quality or Quantity of Work

A new employee may be deficient in the quantity and quality of the work produced, but at the same time he may be punctual and regular in attendance and cooperative and friendly with his co-workers and his supervisor. In this case, the most likely reason is either a lack of job knowledge or no aptitude for the work. A supervisor who is thoroughly familiar with the work can usually make this determination without difficulty. The important thing for the supervisor to decide is whether the deficiency is due to a lack of specific job knowledge that can be acquired during a training period or whether it is caused by a lack of basic intelligence and aptitudes. If he decides that job knowledge is the deficiency, he should establish a definite training period at the end of which the employee should be proficient. If the lack of basic intelligence or necessary aptitude is the problem, no amount of training can overcome it. Basic intelligence is very difficult for a supervisor to assess, but if the employee is unable to follow instructions or to learn the tasks of the job, the problem is much too difficult for the average supervisor to handle. He would be wise not to retain the employee.

A supervisor familiar with the work should know

what basic aptitudes are required. Accounting or statistical jobs require an aptitude for manipulating numbers and for seeing relationships between numbers. If an employee cannot readily see that 2 is 50 percent of 4—if he would be just as likely to figure that 2 is 5 percent of 4—he should not be placed in any job that involves working with numbers.

Jobs that involve a great deal of writing, as many research jobs do, require basic writing and verbal abilities. If an employee cannot write a paragraph that is organized, coherent, and understandable, he should not be placed in a job where writing is essential no matter what other qualifications he may have. Many employees perform poorly on jobs because they lack the basic aptitude for them. The supervisor should immediately try out a new employee in situations that would reveal his aptitude for the work. If he clearly lacks it, he will never be satisfactory. And the sooner he and the supervisor recognize this fact, the better off they both will be. It is far more desirable, in fact, to make the necessary assessment of aptitudes *before* an employee is hired and placed on the job.

When a long-term employee lacks the job knowledge or basic intelligence or aptitude required for the work, the supervisor has a very different problem. These deficiencies are the result of poor hiring practices and poor supervision in the past. Frequently, a new supervisor will find a few of these employees when he takes over a new unit. In fact, the previous supervisor may tell him that a certain employee is a poor performer. The new supervisor should start afresh and make his own evaluations of every employee under him. He may find that his assessments differ substantially from those of his predecessor.

It seems incredible that an employee who has been on the job for many years could lack the aptitudes or the knowledge to perform the work satisfactorily. However, such situations do occur. A new supervisor should work closely with this kind of employee to determine exactly what the problem is. Then he should try to correct it. The employee may simply have lost his interest and enthusiasm for the job. He may have been ignored and bypassed by his supervisor for years. He may have been repeatedly passed over for promotion. Some supervisors are overly hasty in making negative evaluations of an employee's potential. Sometimes they write off the employee and shunt him to the side, out of the mainstream of work. They may go so far as to give him no assignments at all but may let him atrophy while he continues to come to work each day, to put in his time, and to collect his pay check. Or else they may let him occupy his time and mind with inconsequential details.

No supervisor has a right to handle any employee in this fashion. It is a cruel way to treat a human being, and it is grossly unfair to the organization that is paying for services it is not receiving. Not every employee can be a star, and not everyone can advance to positions of greater responsibility. But a supervisor has a clear obligation to develop each employee to the fullest extent possible and to make sure that the employee is contributing to the organization. A new supervisor may find that attention and encouragement can work wonders in bringing the employee out of his shell and in improving his performance.

On occasion, some supervisors use this same technique of isolating an employee and taking all work away from him in the hope that the employee will resign. The strategy frequently fails when the employee does not resign.

At the very least, it is a subterfuge that betrays the supervisor's lack of skill and honesty in dealing with employees.

Performance that for years has been above average may deteriorate because of advancing age or illness or accident. If the employee has had years of service, the situation should be handled as sympathetically as possible. If the deterioration appears to be permanent, the assignment to less demanding duties is the best answer. It is unfair to the employee and to the organization alike to retain the employee in a job that he can no longer perform adequately.

Tardiness and Absenteeism

Sometimes an employee is a good producer but is often tardy or absent from work. There may be several reasons for his behavior. Lax supervision may be a primary reason. If absenteeism or tardiness is tolerated by a supervisor, it will become worse and worse. In a large unit especially, once it starts and is permitted, it will spread like an epidemic.

Overstaffing is another practice that frequently results in absenteeism. If an employee knows that he will be an extra person or that he will have little or nothing to do at work, he will be inclined to stay at home, especially if he does not feel well or if the weather is bad.

Tardiness or absenteeism may simply be a matter of poor work habits. The best approach for a supervisor to take is one of firm discipline. He should make it clear to new employees that punctuality and regular attendance are required, and he should enforce the policy. Docking employees who are frequently tardy often serves as a deterrent.

Some women employees who have small children may be absent frequently because of the children's illnesses or because of baby sitter problems. While an occasional absence is excusable, frequent occurrences should not be condoned. It is unfair to other employees to have one set of rules for them and another set for the mothers of small children. The employee should understand that she has an obligation to her job and that it is her responsibility to work out her family situation satisfactorily.

Supervisors may believe that they have to tolerate frequent breaches of office discipline when the labor market is tight and trained employees are hard to find, or when employees are protected by civil service regulations or a union agreement. This is not the case. Lax discipline makes for poor morale and poor employee relations. Sometimes the notion is advanced that the way to reduce absenteeism or tardiness is to reward employees for regular attendance and punctuality. It has been advocated that employees be paid a bonus for unused sick leave or that unused sick leave (or a portion of it) be added to vacations. This practice would seem highly dubious from a motivational standpoint. Regular attendance and adherence to the established working hours are conditions of employment, and there is no justification for rewarding employees merely for doing what they are supposed to do. It is far more desirable for the supervisor to establish discipline and high standards and to see that they are maintained.

Interpersonal Friction

Some employees work well with people, while others are much more productive when they work alone. These differences are usually accommodated by careful placement of employees on jobs for which they are best suited temperamentally. Other kinds of interpersonal friction, however, can be much more difficult to handle. Extreme hostility and lack of cooperation, temper tantrums, outbursts of rage (often over trivial occurrences), unusual agitation and nervousness (especially under pressure) are kinds of behavior that can be highly disturbing to an organization. Some employees cannot work under pressure. When faced with an unusually heavy workload or a short time deadline, they may become extremely excited and upset and fly into a rage, yelling and screaming and insulting anyone who happens to get in the way. These employees should not be in jobs that have a lot of pressure, especially when pressure is combined with responsibility for dealing with the public. An occasional outburst may be understood and overlooked by a fellow employee, but it will not be by a client who feels that he has been insulted.

A lack of cooperation sometimes indicates that the employee feels threatened by what he is being asked to do. Perhaps he cannot see any sense or value in the request. An overly defined job structure with narrowly defined boundaries between jobs can be a major cause of uncooperativeness. The lack of cooperation in many cases really masks a jurisdictional dispute over job responsibilities and prerogatives.

Chronic interpersonal friction can be a symptom of serious emotional problems. Its handling requires a great deal of alertness and skill on the part of the supervisor.

Emotions and Emotional Illness

So far this discussion has dealt primarily with problems that are relatively straightforward and whose causes are rooted in the job itself or in fairly commonplace situations. Some of the most intractable performance problems, however, have causes that are obscure and very difficult to identify. Emotional disturbances of all kinds frequently interfere with good performance. The most difficult task facing the supervisor is to recognize when poor performance is due to an emotional disturbance rather than to job-related factors. Once he has recognized the fact, then he must try to assess whether the disturbance is temporary or whether the employee needs professional help.

One of the most clear-cut signs of emotional disturbance is an unexplained change for the worse in an employee's performance, moods, or behavior. An employee who has been an above-average performer may start making many mistakes, turning out sloppy work, or not getting the work done at all. Frequently his performance will deteriorate in other ways as well. He may start having frequent absences or coming to work late or leaving early. He may become withdrawn and sullen and begin to have all kinds of difficulties with co-workers when previously he had been pleasant, cheerful, and co-operative.

Temporary periods of great emotional stress can produce these symptoms. There may be a critical illness in the employee's family. His wife or another loved one may have died. He may be extremely upset over financial or other problems. He may be having acute marital trouble. Physical problems can have similar effects. The employee may have developed a physical disorder that is affecting his health and, consequently, his performance. Or he may be emotionally upset about the recent discovery of an illness.

The supervisor may or may not know what is troubling the employee. He should not intrude into the employee's personal affairs, but he should have a frank talk with him. He might ask him if he wants to talk about whatever is bothering him. The supervisor should show concern for the employee, who will probably let him know the nature of the problem even if he prefers not to divulge all of the details.

If the employee is going through a temporary period of great emotional stress, especially that caused by a serious illness or a death in the family, the supervisor should bear with him and give him the necessary emotional support and understanding needed to help him through. Emotional disturbances that become chronic or begin to take on a serious aspect need to be handled in an entirely different way. For example, if the employee continues to have chronic marital difficulties that adversely affect his performance, there is a limit to how long a supervisor can tolerate the situation.

Bizarre behavior that continues over a prolonged period, such as violent outbursts, irrational talk, unusual excitement, and suspected excessive drinking, should be taken as a symptom of emotional illness. The main task of the supervisor is to try to get the employee to seek professional help. This is often difficult because the employee may be reluctant to admit he has a problem.

The supervisor should inform higher management of a problem of this kind, because the employee's behavior may be a threat to the entire organization. The supervisor should also obtain professional advice before initiating any action with the employee. If there is no psychologist or psychiatrist within the organization, he might contact the local mental health association or mental health clinic. If the employee's performance is disruptive, the supervisor should insist that he seek professional help, and he should make continued employment contingent upon such help.

Likewise, when deteriorating performance apparently is due to a physical disorder, the supervisor should require the employee to have a medical examination or to consult a physician for treatment.

John B. Miner cautions against supervisors becoming too involved with their employees' personal problems. A somewhat impersonal relationship is the preferred one between supervisor and subordinate. The relationship should not become similar to the doctor-patient one. A supervisor should not pry into the employee's personal affairs, nor should he encourage the employee to tell him all about his problems. If the employee seeks to do so, it would be better for the supervisor to urge him to go to a more appropriate listener. Being privy to the employee's deepest problems and thoughts would place a heavy burden on the supervisor. In addition, the employee under stress might reveal more than he wanted to about his personal life. He might later regret having told so much and might feel guilty and embarrassed in the supervisor's presence. A strained, awkward relationship would develop between the two, further impairing the work situation.*

Alcoholism

Alcoholism is fairly prevalent in large organizations. It is a form of emotional illness and is often very difficult to identify. Once identification is made, it is hard to get the alcoholic to recognize his problem and seek treatment.

* For a thorough discussion of the unsatisfactory employee, see John B. Miner, *The Management of Ineffective Performance*, McGraw-Hill Book Company, New York, 1963.

An employee's excessive drinking off the job becomes a matter of concern to the supervisor when it adversely affects his performance, his attention to duty, or his interpersonal relations on the job. Drinking *on* the job, in most organizations, is cause for immediate dismissal.

One might suspect alcoholism if an employee's performance and interest begin to deteriorate; if he is frequently absent, especially before and after weekends or holidays; if he spends excessive time away from his desk or machine; and if he takes extended lunch hours. His breath odor and appearance might also be highly indicative of heavy drinking.

If the supervisor is not sure what the problem is, he should have a frank discussion with the employee about his deteriorating performance and should insist that he seek help. If he is sure of a drinking problem, he should be very firm with the employee. He should talk "cold turkey" to him and adopt a strict, no-nonsense attitude toward his drinking. The worst thing a supervisor can do is to support an alcoholic employee by sympathizing with him, by accepting excuses for his drinking, or by stringing along with his promises to do better. If all other efforts fail and performance remains poor, Miner advocates placing the employee on strict probation for a specified period of time, with the understanding that he will be terminated if there is a failure to improve. If the performance difficulties continue during the probationary period, the man should be fired. The shock of hitting bottom may serve as a motive for seeking treatment. Miner suggests that at the time of firing, the man should be told that he will be taken back when and if he can demonstrate that alcoholism will no longer interfere with his performance. This is an important incentive to cure in many cases.

Transferring Employees

Transferring an unsatisfactory employee to another job or another unit is an acceptable solution only when the individual's abilities and aptitudes are not suited to a particular job, and there is good reason to believe that he will perform better in another kind of work.

Transfer is sometimes used by supervisors as a means of getting rid of a problem by passing it on to another, unsuspecting supervisor. Some organizations shunt problem employees from unit to unit and from supervisor to supervisor in the hope that somehow the problem will be solved. This is a futile and wasteful policy that solves nothing. It merely perpetuates the retention of unsatisfactory employees in the organization. Employees whose poor work performance is due to emotional problems or alcoholism may suffer further harm from being passed from supervisor to supervisor. If all efforts by their present supervisors to help them fail, the only sensible action is to terminate their employment.

The Merits of Prevention

A great many of the problems that have been discussed could be prevented by careful prehiring screening. In most cases, lack of job knowledge or basic intelligence or aptitudes can be detected before selection. Potential problems of absenteeism and tardiness resulting from domestic situations can be eliminated by asking questions about the family situations. Working mothers should be asked what provisions they have made for child care or about possible transportation problems to and from work. Many severe cases of emotional illness or alcoholism are readily apparent during an employment interview or can be detected by a careful evaluation and verification of the applicant's previous work history.

Supervisors are not in the business of rehabilitating people. They have neither the time nor the training for it. They should take all steps possible to avoid these situations, which can make their jobs so unpleasant and which can be so costly and disruptive to an organization.

Some mistakes in hiring are, of course, inevitable. Even so, the early months of employment are the appropriate times for a supervisor to test and observe employees and to be sure they will work out satisfactorily. This is the purpose of a formal probationary period, where one is in use. When the training period shows that the employee has serious problems in learning and understanding the work or in getting along with his coworkers, or when it reveals that he has severe emotional problems, he should be terminated.

When Discharge Is Inevitable

The probationary period is the ideal time to test employees and to weed out those who will not be satisfactory. It is always more difficult to discharge an employee who has had several years of service. Nevertheless, this action is sometimes necessary when performance has deteriorated beyond repair, when the employee has become alcoholic, or when he has developed other behavior patterns that make it impossible to help him. The supervisor should not shrink from discharge when it is called for, but he should handle it as tactfully and as humanely as possible.

Many large organizations, civil service systems, and

union contracts have an established procedure for giving employees official warning and for instituting termination action. In the absence of such procedural requirements, the supervisor should follow a sequence of verbal discussion, written warning, and notice of termination. He should first have a frank discussion with the employee in which he points out deficiencies and ways to overcome them and gives the employee a specified time in which to bring his performance up to an acceptable level. The supervisor should keep a written record of this conversation. If the verbal warning fails to produce an improvement in performance, he should then give the employee a written, formal notice that improvement is required by a certain date and that in the absence of such improvement, a termination notice will follow. If the employee's performance does not improve by the required date, the termination notice should be sent immediately.

Some supervisors believe it is preferable to call employees into the office, tell them they are fired, and give them the required amount of separation pay rather than permit them to serve out the notice period. This procedure is frequently used in discharging middle- or upper-level employees. The reason is that supervisors believe it would be disruptive to have the discharged employee remain on the job for a period of several weeks.

While this view may be valid in some circumstances, other considerations outweigh its merits. Discharge is a very painful experience for anyone, and it is better to soften the blow as much as possible. It is only fair that the supervisor discuss the employee's deficiencies with him, give him a chance to improve, and prepare him for the ultimate discharge. As a result of this interview, the employee may see that he and the job are mismatched, and he may voluntarily resign. The discussion may also have unexpected results. It is possible that the employee never before really understood what was expected of him, and he may improve his performance dramatically. If the employee simply lacks the ability that the job demands, or if there is friction between him and the supervisor, it is often desirable to give him a reasonable amount of time to find another job and then let him resign. It is far better to have discharged employees leave an organization with a feeling of goodwill. A discharge that comes without prior warning is always a bitter blow to the employee's pride, and it will leave him with deep resentment toward the supervisor and the organization.

None of the discussion so far applies to what are commonly called discharges for cause. An entirely different situation prevails when an employee is fired for theft, falsification of records, immoral conduct, or the like. In virtually every organization, these acts are grounds for firing on the spot without notice. The employee should not be permitted to remain in the organization a single day after being discharged under these circumstances.

8

Employee Appraisal

*C*ONTINUOUS EVALUATION OF PERFORMANCE
is an essential part of supervision. It is the supervisor's
responsibility to know the talents, strengths, and weaknesses of his employees. Yet employee appraisal is viewed
by many supervisors and by many organizations as a
separate and distinct function. Most large companies and
other organizations have some formal system of periodic
employee evaluation. It would be difficult, however, to
find a system that really worked or that had the confidence of management, supervisors, and employees.

Most supervisors regard the preparation of performance reports as one of their most burdensome tasks. The
reports themselves are frequently meaningless and inaccurate. They often generate suspicion and hostility on the
part of employees. Rarely do they serve the purpose for

which they were intended. There are several reasons for this. For one thing, a formal performance report requires the supervisor to commit to writing his opinion of the employee. He must formulate his evaluation in unequivocal terms. For another, he must appraise his subordinates in terms of specific, predetermined factors of performance, which may not correspond with the way he thinks about the employees.

Problems Inherent in Appraisals

Supervisors often have vague, intuitive, and sometimes ambiguous feelings about the worth of their subordinates. Often a boss will appraise an employee by saying, "Jim is one of my best men—he has real potential." But when asked about *specific* aspects of Jim's performance—particularly his strengths and weaknesses—he will be at a loss and may finally admit that he really does not know much about Jim. He may have observed that Jim is an industrious worker who always turns in his completed assignments on time. On the basis of this single observation, he may rate Jim's *total* performance as above average. He may even say, "Jim is a terrific employee. Give him an assignment and you don't have to worry about its getting done—and on time too." He may have overlooked the fact that the *quality* of Jim's work is poor; that he frequently comes to unsupported and faulty conclusions; that he is not careful in his work and is inclined to omit important details; and that his interpersonal relations are barely acceptable. The common tendency to project the evaluation of a single observed trait into a *total* evaluation of a person's performance is known as the *halo effect*. It is a major weakness in formal appraisal systems. A more accurate evaluation of Jim might have been: above average in industriousness and quantity of work; below average in quality, in soundness of judgment and analytical ability; and below average in interpersonal relations. Quite a different picture!

Another tendency is to rate all employees right down the middle; that is, to rate them all average or acceptable. In effect, this is no evaluation at all, since it does not differentiate the strengths and weaknesses of individual employees. It is a lazy approach or an easy way out, because it avoids the need for the supervisor to give serious thought to each person.

A number of attempts have been made to overcome these various problems through design of the rating form or system. For example, much research has gone into the *forced-choice* method, which attempts to overcome bias and the halo effect by requiring the supervisor to choose between two or more equally attractive statements as being most descriptive of the employee being rated. Since the supervisor does not know which of the statements has the higher score, he is forced to think about specific instances of the employee's behavior and to ignore his general, overall impression of the employee. At least, that is the theory underlying the method.

Some experts believe that check lists or rating scales are more objective; others prefer a narrative form on which the supervisor is required to write an evaluation of each employee in his own words. The plain truth is that *any* rating form or system is only as good as the supervisors who are doing the ratings. It is impossible for a rating system to overcome supervisor bias, because rating *is* the supervisor's judgment of an employee. If a supervisor does not know the work, or if he does not take the time to become familiar with specific aspects of an employee's performance, he cannot possibly make a valid rating.

A more subtle influence on performance appraisal is a supervisor's tendency to evaluate his subordinates in terms of his own ego needs and the way the subordinates meet those needs. A supervisor cannot shed his own personality when he appraises his employees. We have already discussed the type of individual who could not delegate real responsibility because he gained great ego satisfaction from trying to do everything himself. He became involved in every detail and made every decision. This person would naturally surround himself with men who were passive and submissive and who did not initiate action or make decisions. This kind of subordinate would meet precisely the personality needs of his supervisor, and the supervisor would give him a very high performance rating.

We also discussed the case of a technically incompetent supervisor who surrounded himself with people less competent than he, who looked up to him, and who did not recognize his inadequacies. We can be sure that this kind of supervisor would give this kind of subordinate a very high performance rating. The complex interrelationship between the egos and personalities of supervisors and subordinates is probably the real reason most appraisal systems fail. Evaluations cannot really be objective. They need to be discounted, deflated, or inflated by some coefficient that represents the competence and personality of the supervisor. No way has been discovered to do this, and probably none ever will be.

A debatable point in performance evaluation is whether the employee should see his rating. Appraisals that are not disclosed to the employee unquestionably are more frank, especially with respect to the employee's weaknesses. Many supervisors dislike intensely the idea of telling an employee what his weaknesses are. If the employee's job is covered by a union contract, the supervisor is often afraid that an unfavorable performance rating will result in a grievance.

Of course, an employee will rarely overcome his weaknesses unless they are pointed out to him. If helping the employee improve is one of the purposes of an appraisal, its contents obviously must be disclosed to him. Furthermore, performance appraisals are often used as a basis for such administrative actions as promotions, pay increases, demotions, and discharges. In these cases, it is unethical for a supervisor to give an employee a rating that will have unfavorable consequences without disclosing the rating to him. Most civil service systems and union contracts provide for ratings to be discussed with the employees. Often the employee is required to read and sign the rating sheet.

Requirements of an Effective System

To be effective, an appraisal system should be simple and straightforward. It should attempt to measure employees against factors which the organization has predetermined to be the most essential for success. A great deal of thought should go into selecting the factors, which might well vary for different classes of work. Professional and managerial jobs have far different performance requirements from semiskilled or unskilled work. Quantity and quality of work and technical knowledge are factors that apply across the board to all kinds of jobs, and they form the nucleus for most rating systems.

The factors used should be clearly observable in the employee's work. They should apply to all jobs in the same class of work. They should mean the same thing to everyone. And they should be clearly distinguishable from each other. *Observable, universal,* and *distinguishable;* these are the three criteria that each factor should meet. Personality or character traits, such as *flexibility, adaptability, attitude, trustworthiness,* and *open-mindedness,* are factors that should *not* be used because they are ambiguous and subject to various interpretations. Also, the supervisor may have no objective way of evaluating these qualities by observing the employee's work performance. *Leadership potential* is another subjective factor that often finds its way into a performance rating form. Its use encourages supervisors to render off-the-cuff opinions of employees on the basis of very little knowledge.

Ratings should not be required so often that they constitute a real burden to the supervisor. During the first year of employment, ratings should be made several times. After that, once a year is sufficient.

Narrative or free-form appraisals are rarely satisfactory, especially if the supervisor has many employees to rate. They are inconsistent in the amount of factual information they contain, depending upon the supervisor's writing ability or the amount of time he cares to devote to them. They often tell absolutely nothing significant about an employee's performance. Some supervisors are inclined to write flowery reports on employees they like or whom they want to promote. Furthermore, a supervisor may attempt to disguise his lack of real knowledge about the employee's performance by writing reams of generalities.

Supervisors normally do not control the kind of

rating form or system used in their organizations. However, they are certainly in an excellent position to recommend changes or improvements in a system that they believe is ineffective or unduly cumbersome. The active interest and involvement of supervisors could dramatically improve many systems.

A supervisor should recognize performance appraisals for what they really are—a written reflection of the relationship between the supervisor and the employee. If the supervisor is unable to make a definitive appraisal of the work of a subordinate, he is not discharging his full responsibility. If an unsatisfactory written appraisal comes as a shock to the employee, there is something drastically wrong in the supervisory relationship. Each employee should be kept informed on a continuing basis of how well he is doing, what his weak spots are, and how he can improve them. This is the essence of supervision. Once this kind of relationship has been established, the performance rating becomes a written record that confirms the understanding between supervisor and subordinate.

Performance Requirements

Some organizations have attempted to overcome problems inherent in appraisals by developing a system of performance requirements. Underlying the system is the belief that one cannot evaluate performance objectively without knowing exactly what performance is required or expected. The first essential, therefore, is to figure out and write down in specific language the kind of performance and the type of results that are expected. Actual performance can then be measured against them.

Although the principle is plausible, the practice of writing performance requirements for each job is rarely successful—except in two instances. One is in straight production jobs where expected quantity and quality can be determined by time studies and where actual output can be counted easily. The other instance is in the case of certain top management jobs where expected results can be represented by dollar amounts, such as net earnings or gross or net sales.

For most jobs in between these two extremes, written performance requirements do not increase the objectivity or validity of performance ratings. Results expected from jobs are very difficult to establish in specific, quantitative terms. For this reason, supervisors often resort to generalities or abstract phrases, or they go through the motions of preparing performance requirements without devoting a great deal of time or thought to them.

There is a potential benefit in a system of written performance requirements that is often overlooked. If the employee is an active participant, the process of establishing goals and expected results can be a very good tool for training and development. It forces the employee to think about the different parts of his job, what he can reasonably accomplish, and what should be required of him. The supervisor can use the process to push the employee into setting higher goals for himself and for assuming greater responsibility. This use is much more appropriate for middle- and upper-level employees whose jobs afford them opportunity for independent action and decision than it is for employees on a lower level or in unskilled jobs.

The same thing can be said for the concepts of managing by objectives or results, which have gained popularity in recent years. In certain situations, there is value in having subordinates establish objectives to be accomplished within a specified time and then measuring actual accomplishment against these objectives. This tool of supervision can be useful in professional or managerial jobs where the employee has considerable independence in establishing goals, planning his work, and undertaking new programs. It is inappropriate for routine, repetitive, or production type of work or for stuctured jobs in which the employee is responsible for performing assigned duties. Whenever the method is used, it should be kept extremely simple, and elaborate reporting systems should be avoided. The setting of objectives and the measurement of accomplishments should take place through personal interaction between supervisor and subordinate.

Counseling Employees on Performance

Appraising an employee's performance is only one-half of a rating system. The other half is informing the employee of the evaluation in such a way that he will be motivated toward continued improvement and accomplishment. The literature on supervision has made much of the appraisal interview. This is the conversation between supervisor and subordinate in which the supervisor discusses the employee's performance with him, including his strengths, his weaknesses, and how he can improve. Much has been written regarding the techniques a supervisor should use in this interview, so that he presents the employee with a balanced picture of his performance, praising his strengths and pointing out weaknesses in such a way that the employee will want to improve and will leave the interview with renewed loyalty, dedication, and confidence in himself and his supervisor.

The appraisal interview is often presented as so formidable and so crucial to the supervisor-employee relationship that even the most confident supervisors and subordinates approach it with foreboding. But, if the supervisory relationship is what it should be, all of this to-do about the appraisal interview is unnecessary. As we have said before, a supervisor has a clear obligation to keep an employee informed of his progress on a continuing basis. Everything that appears in the performance rating should already be known to the employee. Most systems provide for annual ratings. Surely a supervisor cannot wait until then to form his opinion of the employee's performance or to let the employee know whether he is satisfactory.

The Value of Praise

It is just as important to let an employee know when he is performing well as it is to call attention to his deficiencies. Many supervisors find it difficult to praise employees in their work, just as many individuals find it hard to pay compliments to others in their social lives. They feel embarrassed and awkward. They think it is undignified or demeaning to their status. Nothing, of course, could be further from the truth.

The judicious use of praise can be a very powerful tool for motivating employees. Praise should not be fulsome; nor should it be offered for mediocre or routine performance. But when an employee works very hard and does an especially good job, he should know that the boss recognizes and appreciates his efforts. "This is a very thorough report, Bob"; or "You handled thàt negotiation very well"; or "You did a fine job of meeting that deadline, Mary." These are simple, sincere statements that speak volumes to the employee concerned. Many meek, withdrawn, and unsure employees have been brought out of their shells and developed into effective workers by supervisors perceptive enough to recognize their good qualities and skillful in using praise and encouragement to build their self-confidence. Unfortunately, too many highly motivated employees who try hard to do an outstanding job have become disheartened and thwarted by supervisors who never praise their accomplishments but do carp on their mistakes.

To be effective, praise should be timely. It should be given when something occurs that merits it. It should *never* be saved until a later time and then used to soften criticism of the employee. "You did a fine job of meeting that deadline three months ago, Mary, but I want to talk to you about your spelling. I found three misspelled words in these letters today and this isn't the first time I have noticed it." By this time, Mary is probably wondering *what* deadline she met three months ago. Anyway, the praise is making no impression on her because of her anxiety over the criticism of her spelling.

A favorable written appraisal can motivate an above-average employee to further effort. Even though their individual accomplishments may be praised, employees are never completely sure of how they stack up over all. It is rewarding to them to read performance reports that rate them highly in most respects and that show a high regard for their value to the organization. A further gratification is the fact that the favorable reports become a part of the permanent personnel record.

Discussing Employees' Deficiencies

Most supervisors believe one of their most difficult tasks is the discussion of performance weaknesses with employees. Sometimes they avoid this task altogether, or they couch the discussion in such evasive language that its impact on the employee is slight. Performance problems should be pointed out when they occur. If the supervisor waits until some later date when a performance rating is due and then tries to discuss the deficiency, the employee may not know what he is talking about. He may have forgotten the incident entirely. Even if he remembers it, he may be unable to understand what he did wrong because no mention of it was made at the time.

Supervisors should not be too hesitant about showing displeasure at performance that is grossly unacceptable, especially if the failure is willful or due to neglect. Over the years, supervisors have been fed a great deal of human relations theory that presents the supervisor-subordinate relationship as a delicate and fragile thing that can easily be destroyed by a misspoken word or an ill-timed act on the supervisor's part. According to this view, a supervisor must keep a tight rein on his emotions at all times in order to preserve the goodwill of his employees. He should not let them know that he is furious with them or that he thinks they are performing miserably. Much of this philosophy is nonsense, and it does an injustice to both parties and to their relationship.

Suppose a sales manager is deluged with letters and telephone calls from customers in a particular sales territory, complaining that the goods they ordered two months ago were never delivered. After checking into the matter, he finds that Jack, the salesman, never turned in the orders. Unless Jack is a brand-new employee who does not realize the importance of sending in orders immediately, the sales manager should let Jack know of his displeasure immediately in no uncertain terms. His main concern should be to make sure that the performance breach is not repeated, and his reprimand to Jack should be strong enough to make an impression.

Some proponents of the human relations school of thought have advised supervisors to handle an employee's performance violation by calling in the entire group of employees, telling them that there has been a violation but not saying by whom, and asking the entire group to be sure it does not happen again. The idea is that the actual violator will "get the message" without having the embarrassment of being called to task by his supervisor.

If the case just mentioned had been handled this way, instead of reprimanding Jack individually the sales manager would have sent a memorandum to the whole sales staff telling them of the occurrence (but not saying who committed the error) and admonishing them all to send in their orders promptly. Hopefully, Jack would read the memorandum and would heed it.

This method of handling a performance problem is wrong. It is usually ineffective because the employee at fault does not take the group warning seriously. It is also unfair to reprimand the employees who are not involved in the incident. It weakens the supervisor in the eyes of the employees (including the offender) because they think he lacks the courage to speak directly to the person at fault. A supervisor enhances rather than jeopardizes his relationship with his subordinates by dealing with each individual honestly and frankly and by letting them know when he is dissatisfied with their performance. Employees like to know where they stand with a supervisor. They would rather be treated as mature, responsible adults than be handled with kid gloves by a supervisor who is afraid to confront them with anything unpleasant.

Dealing with individual employees openly and frankly, however, does not mean that the supervisor has a license to blow up at the slightest provocation, to yell and scream at employees, or to browbeat them. Neither does he have the right to throw temper tantrums if he fails to get his way.

If an employee commits an error, no matter how serious, the supervisor should not humiliate him by bawling him out in public. The supervisor should concentrate his displeasure on the *error* the employee has committed. He should not make his criticism a *personal* attack on the employee's worth as a human being. He never has the right to use abusive or profane language in reprimanding an employee.

Consistency is a great virtue in supervisors. Their standards of performance should be consistent. They should not tolerate or overlook sloppy work one week and then become angry over the same quality of work the next week. Their treatment of employees also should be consistent. They should not reprimand employees over minor infractions one time and be friendly and understanding the next time the same errors are committed. Supervisors who have wide swings in mood from day to day are very difficult to work for. Employees are continually trying to figure out what mood the boss is in at a given time, and they may avoid him as much as possible because of his unpredictability.

"Let the punishment fit the crime" is an old saying that is especially apt in the handling of performance problems. A supervisor should judge not only the seriousness of errors or poor decisions but also their likely causes. New employees may make errors or neglect important details because they do not understand the work. In this case, the supervisor should certainly tell them of the deficiency, but he should try to correct it by training. It does little good to give the employee a severe reprimand. An employee may do poor work because he lacks a necessary skill. It does little good to criticize a poor typist; she no doubt is doing the best she can. Training is the only thing likely to help. An employee may not have the aptitude or the mental ability to do a certain kind of work. Reprimanding him will not improve his performance. It may make him so fearful that he will perform even more poorly.

A severe reprimand is in order when a supervisor is sure that the employee's performance is poor because he is lazy, because he does not apply himself, or because he is indifferent. He should be made to understand that he is expected to improve and that the present quality of his work will not be tolerated.

The personality of the employee is an important factor in deciding the appropriate action to take. Some employees are so eager to please and so upset when they make errors that merely calling mistakes to their attention is all that is necessary. A harsh scolding might be devastating to them. Others are so thick-skinned that nothing short of a strong reprimand will make any impression.

The relationship between supervisor and employee also has a bearing on the approach that will be most effective. Some men will accept with good grace an angry bawling out from a man supervisor whom they respect, but a great many men will consider a harsh reprimand from any woman supervisor a blow to their self-respect. Most women employees become upset if they are "raked over the coals" in an angry tone of voice by their supervisor, regardless of whether the supervisor is a man or a woman.

It is wise to take all of these factors into account when dealing with performance problems. The supervisor's primary objective should be to improve the performance and to correct whatever deficiency there is. He should take an approach that is most likely to achieve these results. Above all, a reprimand should never be so bitter or so personal that it becomes a permanent barrier between supervisor and employee. The supervisor should not continue to hold the deficiency against the employee, nor should he remind him of it at a later time. Once the problem is corrected it should be forgotten, and both the supervisor and the employee should move on to other things.

9

Selection and Training

$\mathcal{M}$ANY PERFORMANCE PROBLEMS CAN BE
avoided by selecting new employees carefully, by training
them properly, and by observing their progress during
the early months of employment. Selection and training
go hand in hand; if one is deficient, the other cannot succeed. No amount of training can make a good worker out
of a person who lacks basic intelligence, aptitude, or motivation or who is generally unsuited to the work. Likewise,
the best selection practices may be nullified by a lack of
follow-up, training, or direction.

Poor selection has several causes. Foremost is the failure to identify sufficiently the specific knowledge, skills,
aptitude, and temperament required by the job. A great
deal of hiring takes the form of recruiting bodies to fill
vacant positions. The major effort goes into filling the

job as speedily as possible. It is pure luck if the recruits turn out well. Another cause of poor selection is the failure to find out enough about an applicant during the pre-employment interview or to make the right evaluation of those facts that were discovered. The third cause is a failure to make an adequate verification of an applicant's stated education and work history.

Supervisors in organizations of any size usually do not have to do all of their own recruiting for staff. They have a personnel department to help them, although they may have leads and contacts of their own. However, personnel department interviewers often have only the haziest idea of what the duties of a job are or the kind of individual the job requires. Consequently, their screening process cannot be highly refined. They merely look for applicants who meet very general requirements of education and experience and leave the responsibility for making a definitive selection to the supervisor. If the supervisor tends to accept any applicant who makes a fairly decent appearance, it is inevitable that numerous mistakes in hiring will occur. In addition, if the supervisor is inclined to pay little attention to the training and development of his staff, a poor employment selection can easily grow into a full-blown performance problem. The supervisor may not even be aware of it until the employee's behavior becomes so unacceptable or his performance so deficient that serious disruptions to the work result.

Professional men, such as physicians, lawyers, or small businessmen who recruit and hire their employees directly, often pay too little attention to the kind of skills, aptitudes, and personalities the jobs require. They devote too little time to careful interviewing of applicants and to verification of their work histories before hiring them. They frequently rely on employment agencies to do their screening and selecting, or they may ask a friend to recommend someone for the vacant position.

The job itself is the starting point for good hiring of personnel. The supervisor knows more than anyone else about the job. He should carefully analyze its major duties and decide on the qualifications it requires. He should insure that the employment interviewer knows these requirements, and together they should decide on the kind of person to be recruited.

Training and experience requirements should not be prescribed so narrowly that they rule out promising applicants who could handle the job. Many jobs can be performed by individuals with a fairly wide range of backgrounds. For example, a supervisor looking for a secretary should not limit his recruiting to individuals who are now working as executive secretaries. A present stenographer might have excellent potential for the job. The recruitment effort should concentrate on those qualifications that are truly essential. In this case, they might well be good typing and shorthand skills; knowledge of filing and office practices; proficiency in punctuation, spelling, and grammar; a pleasant personality and good appearance; alertness; and an ability to follow through on a variety of details and to work without supervision.

Educational qualifications are sometimes set unrealistically high. It would be foolish to recruit a professional accountant to fill a job that involved routine posting to the general ledger and that could be performed by a clerk with a knowledge of bookkeeping. It would be wasteful to hire a professional engineer for a routine drafting job. Organizations sometimes recruit college graduates for jobs that could be handled by clerks.

In many cases, it must be decided if the job requires an individual who already is proficient in a trade or occupation or if the job merely requires an *aptitude* for learning the particular type of work. The supervisor is in the best position to make this evaluation.

Job requirements have several dimensions. In addition to the essential knowledge, skills, training, and aptitudes demanded, they usually require specific personal and emotional qualities. Any employer wants to hire a person who is stable, who is likely to remain with the organization, who will like the work and be interested in it, who will get along well with his co-workers and his supervisor, and who will be regular in attendance and punctuality. Personal appearance, manners, and speaking voice are very important in jobs that deal with the public. Social ability, initiative, and drive can be essential in selling jobs as well as in other kinds of work.

Tools of Selection

There are four basic tools of employment selection: (1) the application forms, (2) preemployment tests, (3) the personal interview, and (4) verification checks with schools and former employers. A good selection procedure integrates all four tools so that they complement each other.

The Application Form

A completed application blank reveals much about a person. It shows whether an individual has the required education and experience. It may reveal a great deal about the person's motivation, drive, maturity, and talents, if the various facts shown are evaluated and fitted together.

Does the applicant's history show steady purpose and progress? Does his job record show advancement in salary and level of responsibility? Does his education reveal definite goals? Does he have family responsibilities that would make steady work essential to him? Or does his work history show an aimless movement from job to job, or even from one kind of work to another with little or no salary progression? Does his education show the same lack of purpose, with little or no relation to the kind of work he has done since? Are there unexplained gaps in his work history? These are all questions that can be answered by a careful analysis of the application blank.

Preemployment Tests

Preemployment tests are controversial. Psychological tests that attempt to measure personality, emotional stability, and interests have been severely criticized for their invasion of privacy as well as for their frequent lack of validity. Similarly, pencil and paper tests that attempt to measure general intelligence, knowledge of a subject, or aptitudes are under heavy attack as discriminating against applicants from deprived backgrounds who lack language skills.

The most valid and useful preemployment tests are those that directly measure skill and aptitude. If a particular skill or aptitude is essential to a job, it should be checked out before an applicant is hired. Failure to do so may prove very costly. Whenever possible, the test should be a sample of the work itself or a task that closely resembles the work and that requires the same skills or aptitudes. An organization does not need to have an elaborate testing program in order to make this determination. An imaginative supervisor can usually give the applicant a brief test of the work during the employment interview.

Any applicant for a typing or stenographic job should be tested before hiring. Applicants' estimates of their typing and shorthand speeds are notoriously inaccurate. It is foolish to hire a typist or stenographer and afterwards find that she cannot type or take dictation and transcribe is accurately or that she is very poor at spelling and grammar. There are a number of timed typing tests on the commercial market that a supervisor can use. However, it is preferable to give the applicant a sample of the work that is done in the office, written in rough draft, and ask her to type it, correcting any misspelled words or grammatical errors and inserting the proper punctuation. This is a more valid test for the job than a commercial typing test. The supervisor may dictate a letter to the applicant for a stenographic job and have her transcribe it in finished letter form. Tests of this kind should be timed, and the length of time an applicant requires to complete it should be compared with an "average time" that the supervisor can establish by having the test taken by several present employees with satisfactory skills.

A supervisor may test for mechanical ability or manual dexterity by giving the applicant a live problem to solve. For example, he may ask the applicant to get a balky mechanical toy to work or to take the toy apart and put it together again. Manual dexterity may be assessed by observing the way the applicant uses hand tools.

If a job requires a great deal of writing, the supervisor should have the applicant write a page or two as part of the interview process. The subject might be on a topic related to the work; or it might be on something of a very general nature. Or the supervisor could let the applicant write on any subject he chooses. He might request him to write a self-evaluation of his strengths and weaknesses as they relate to the job for which he is applying. This kind of essay could reveal much more about the applicant than just his writing skill. The finished piece of writing should be judged for its content and style and also for the length of time required to complete it.

A further advantage of giving a skill test as part of the interview process is that it permits the interviewer to discuss the test results with the applicant. A person who lacks the necessary skill or aptitude for a particular job will usually recognize that fact when he does poorly on this kind of test.

In some cases, it is not possible to test an applicant with an actual sample of the work to be performed. Computer jobs, for example, require a certain aptitude, but it is not practical to try out applicants on the computer. A commercially prepared aptitude test—usually of the pencil and paper variety—has to be used.

The Personal Interview

The preemployment interview should be used to supplement information obtained through the application form and tests. During the interview, a supervisor can usually measure the applicant's technical or professional knowledge of a field by asking him incisive questions and evaluating his responses. He can also evaluate the depth and breadth of the applicant's experience by appropriate questioning. The opportunity an interview gives for evaluating technical knowledge and experience is one of its two major advantages. The other advantage is the opportunity it presents to assess the applicant's personal and emotional characteristics.

Of course, many interviews do not achieve these two purposes. Many are conducted so haphazardly that they are a waste of time. Good interviewing is a skill that can be learned and, once learned, usually pays rich dividends.

√ Good preparation is the first step toward making the interview productive. The application form should be gone over and evaluated before the interview starts. If the prospect brings the completed form with him to the interview, he should be asked to wait while the supervisor has an opportunity to review it privately. Notes should be made of particular areas to be discussed with the applicant, of further information to be obtained, and of items to be verified. There should be a definite purpose and plan to the interview. Many supervisors find it helpful to record the interview summary on a preplanned form, but notes should not be taken during the interview itself. A checklist of information to be obtained from an interview would generally include the following items, the amount of detail varying with the job and the work history of the applicant:

1. *Experience and education.* Does the applicant have the required education and training for the job? How well does he know and understand the work? Has he performed similar duties previously? Has he undertaken progressively more difficult jobs? Does his salary progression indicate increasing responsibility? Does his past work history indicate initiative and drive? Has he had any leadership experience?

2. *Attitude and maturity.* Does his job record indicate steady progress, or has he shifted from job to job with no apparent purpose? Does he have unexplained gaps in his job or education record?

Were his reasons for leaving previous jobs sound, or were they apparently due to poor performance, friction, or similar causes? Does he seem to be easily dissatisfied or discouraged? Did he have sound reasons for leaving school? Did his education relate to the work he has been doing? Is his reaction to questions about his past history defensive or frank? Does he appear genuinely interested in the work applied for? Does he appear to have a well-balanced family life? Does he have family or other responsibilities that are likely to interfere with his performance (consider baby-sitting problems with working mothers)? Does he live within a normal commuting distance from the job? Does he have a history of alcoholism or emotional illness? If so, does his record indicate that he has made a full recovery?

3. *Appearance and personality.* Is he neat and well groomed? How well does he express himself? Are his voice and manner of speaking well suited to the job applied for? Has he had experience in working with the public? How successful was he? How well did he get along with previous supervisors and co-workers? Does he appear to be unusually excitable, nervous, or ill at ease? Does he have any physical disabilities?

The interview process. The interview should be a dynamic exchange between interviewer and applicant. It has two main goals: (1) to inform the applicant of the nature of the work and the job requirements so that he can decide whether he is interested, and (2) to obtain definitive information about the applicant, to be used in evaluating how well qualified he is for the job.

Interviewers frequently do too much talking themselves. They may devote the major part of the interview to discussing the organization, the vacant job, and their own work and never learn anything of significance about the applicant. The best interview usually takes place when the *applicant* does the major share of the talking; when the interviewer skillfully guides the discussion so that the applicant divulges pertinent facts about his previous history and also about his attitudes, emotions, likes, and dislikes.

While the interviewer should be well prepared and should keep in mind his checklist of information to be obtained, he should conduct the interview along conversational lines. He should not fire a barrage of questions at the applicant. Rather, he might quietly inject questions at the appropriate place in the conversation in order to clear up points or to elicit further information. He should phrase his questions in a friendly, affirmative fashion rather than ask them in a way that implies rejection of the applicant. The interviewer is not conducting an inquisition. "Tell me how you believe your past experience prepares you for this job" is a better question and more likely to produce information than, "Why do you think you are qualified?"

The interview usually will proceed more smoothly if a fairly definite sequence is followed. It is trite to say, put the applicant at ease. Nevertheless, it is very important to create a cordial atmosphere for the interview. Most people are tense and somewhat nervous when they begin an employment interview. A few minutes of small talk at the beginning about the weather or about some inconsequential subject will create a more relaxed setting.

The next step is to give the applicant a general orientation to the job and to the organization. He will become more at ease if he can listen for the first part of the interview. It is wise not to go into all the details of the job at this point, and the applicant should not be permitted to divert attention from his background by asking a multitude of questions about the job or the organization.

After the initial orientation, the interview should move on to the main objective, which is to learn as much as possible about the applicant. Start with his education and work history and proceed gradually to more personal areas. Do not start with subjects that are likely to be threatening to the applicant. Leave them for later in the interview, after more rapport has been established. Training and work history are normally the least threatening subjects for early discussion.

As an example, let us assume that you are interviewing an applicant for an accounting job. You have reviewed his application and note that in the ten years since he left college he has held four positions, each involving almost identical duties and each carrying about the same salary. In each case he gave his reason for leaving a company, "to get more experience." You also note that he went to college for three years and that there is an unexplained gap of two years between the year he left college and his first job. He shows his marital status as divorced. A red flag has gone up in your mind. You are concerned about the stability of the man. The information you most want to get out of this interview is what he was doing those two years between college and work and why he has changed jobs so often. However, direct questions on these subjects are not appropriate for beginning the interview. You may not have to ask them at all. If you get the applicant talking freely about his background, he may tell you everything you want to know without being asked.

When you have finished the small-talk and the job-orientation phases of the interview, say simply, "Now, Mr. Smith, suppose you tell me the highlights of your previous experience; what parts were the most difficult, what parts you liked the best, and how you believe they relate to our job here." An open-ended question of this kind should start him going. As he proceeds, you may ask other questions as necessary, such as: "Wasn't your new job very much like your old one? Why did you change? Did you like your supervisor better in the next job? What career had you planned when you went to college? What was your major? Why didn't you graduate?"

An essential part of interviewing is *listening*. Listen intently to everything the applicant tells you and also what he fails to tell you. Observe his reactions as he discusses various areas of his past history. Don't be so preoccupied with what you will ask next that you tune yourself out to what he is saying. Let him follow his own sequence of events as long as he reveals the information you want. Even though your checklist starts with training and work history and has emotional stability and maturity toward the end of the interview, do not interrupt him or fail to listen if he starts in immediately telling you about his divorce, his drinking problem, and the two years he spent in a psychiatric hospital before he started working.

The art of asking questions. Some questions will bring forth valuable information; others will not. A broad, open-ended question, such as, "What qualifications of experience and education do you believe you have that especially fit this job?" will often require the applicant to organize his thoughts before answering. The information he gives and the way he presents it can show a great deal about the way he thinks. It also may reveal things that he wants to conceal or gloss over. This type of question should be used freely in interviews. It often is a good way to get the interview moving after the preliminaries have been completed. It cannot be used exclusively because it does not sufficiently pinpoint information. It should be supplemented with specific questions, asked at appropriate points, to pin down details.

Specific questions asked should make good use of the words what, why, how, who, and when. For example: What were your exact duties? What was your grade average in college? What office machines have you used? Why did you leave that job? Why did you major in history? How would you program a payroll for the computer? How do you multiply and divide on the *Monroe* calculator? Who supervised your work? Who had to give the final O.K. for the project? Who made up the community group with which you worked? When did you graduate? When did you get out of the service?

In trying to assess an applicant's technical knowledge or experience, it is imperative to use questions that require him to call forth specific facts. Ask him to tell you in detail how certain jobs were done. Questions that can be answered yes or no should not be used because they do not elicit the necessary information. For example, suppose some of the previous questions were reworded into the following: Were you an accounting clerk there? Were your grades pretty good in college? Do you know how to program a payroll for the computer? Can you multiply and divide on the *Monroe* calculator? To all of these questions, the applicant could reply yes or no and the interviewer would know no more than he did before the interview started. Ask questions that require the applicant to give definitive, precise answers.

Leading questions that imply the answer described should also be avoided. For example, the question, "You are good at detail, aren't you?" would usually receive a

yes answer. Personal questions should not be asked unless
the information is essential. It is certainly appropriate to
ask about a person's marital status and how many children he has or to ask a woman with small children about
her arrangements for their care. It is not proper to inquire about an applicant's marital relations, unless something in his work background indicates that his domestic
situation was a constant disruption to his work. A young
single girl might well be asked if she has plans to marry
soon, because that fact might bear directly on how long
she remains with the organization. A divorced person
might be asked how long he had been divorced, because a
very recent divorce or one that is not final might have adverse effects on his work. It is inappropriate to ask about
the reasons for the divorce. Inquiry about a person's financial status is not appropriate either, unless his previous
background has revealed chronic debt problems that interfered with his work.

If an applicant is very evasive about his work history,
it may be a good idea to challenge him with a provocative
question, such as, "Would you prefer not to continue the
interview?" The interviewer has to feel his way during
much of the interview and adapt his behavior to the applicant and the circumstances. No two interviews should be
alike. Each applicant is different and the interview should
be oriented toward those differences. A stereotyped, cut-
and-dried set of questions usually produces inferior results.

The primary job of the interviewer is to elicit information that can be evaluated to determine whether the
applicant should be hired for the job. The interviewer
should listen with an open mind to what the applicant says.
He should not antagonize the applicant by arguing with
him; nor should he express disagreement, shock, or dis-

belief at what he hears. If the applicant says that he is an alcoholic or a narcotics addict or that he has served a prison term for robbery, the interviewer should not react. Simply accept the statements for what they are, facts that the applicant is revealing about himself.

Controlling and ending the interview. The interviewer should retain control of the interview at all times, in terms of both the time it is taking and the direction of the conversation. Interviews should not be allowed to drag on and on. If the interviewer is well prepared and keeps the discussion on the track, 20 minutes on the average should be ample time. If an applicant is so taciturn or withdrawn that the interviewer finds it impossible to elicit any information from him, the interview should be terminated after a reasonable effort has been made.

When the interviewer has learned the essential facts about the applicant and in turn has given the applicant information about the job, he should terminate the conversation. Some authorities recommend that the applicant be told then and there whether he is to be considered for the job. In may cases, however, this is an unwise policy from a practical standpoint. If an applicant is clearly unqualified by purely objective standards (for example, if he does not have the specific experience or training required or if he did very badly on a skill or aptitude test), then in most cases the interviewer might tell him that he cannot be considered. For the most part, applicants will accept a rejection gracefully when it is based on grounds of technical qualifications or skill. However, if the applicant's qualifications are borderline or if he is defensive about them, the interviewer should not become involved in a discussion that could lead to an argument about the applicant's background.

When the applicant is unacceptable because of appearance, personality, emotional stability, or other subjective factors in his background, the interviewer should never tell him that he cannot be considered. The applicant may well want to argue the point, and, if he is emotionally unstable, he may become abusive or threatening. He should be told that many more applicants are yet to be interviewed and that if there is a need to talk to him further, he will be contacted. You should not promise to let him know "one way or another" or to let him hear by a certain date.

In most cases, a supervisor does not want to make a final decision on whether to hire an applicant during the interview. Even if an applicant appears very well suited for the job, his past work history should be verified before any final decision is made. Usually, interviews can be terminated by indicating that you have finished the discussion and by thanking the applicant for his time. Or you might rise from your chair to signify that the discussion has ended.

Evaluating the information. If a supervisor has obtained worthwhile facts about an applicant's technical qualifications, he usually has no trouble evaluating them. Personal history information is a very different matter. People are inclined to judge others according to their own set of values and to have stereotyped views on what kinds of backgrounds are predictive of success in a field of work.

For example, the sales manager might have been a college football star. He might view the successful salesman as an individual who played football and went out for other sports in college. He could have a blind spot when he interviews an applicant for a selling job who does not care for sports and who did not engage in them during his college days. Another supervisor might have worked in the organization for many years, and he might unconsciously believe that stability means staying with the same company for ten years or more. He might tend to disqualify an applicant who has had three jobs in the past ten years, even though each job meant far greater responsibility and salary advancement. Another supervisor might have the opposite stereotype in mind. He might believe that rapid movement from job to job indicates a driving, dynamic character. He then might be prejudiced against an applicant who stayed in the same job for many years.

These stereotypes are hard to overcome, for they are a part of human nature. But they can interfere with a supervisor's judgment of a prospective employee and lead him into selection errors. It is wise not to jump to conclusions about applicants. A young man who has changed jobs several times may not have found his right niche, and perhaps this job will be the right one for him. On the other hand, an older man who has accomplished little and has drifted from job to job is certainly not a good prospect so far as stability is concerned. Each applicant should be judged on his own merits, and his *total* background should be weighed in terms of the job to be filled.

Another mistake many supervisors make is to let their sympathy for the applicant distort their judgment. An applicant may obviously be ill-suited for a job and may have severe emotional problems that would be apparent to the most unperceptive, untrained person. The supervisor knows that he should not hire the man, but he sometimes does hire him out of sympathy and in the mistaken belief that he can help him. Misplaced kindness of this sort is an open invitation to years of performance problems. It is unfair to the applicant, who needs professional help, not sympathy. It is more than unfair to the organization and to the other employees.

A supervisor is not required to diagnose emotional or personal problems of an applicant. Diagnosis, in fact, is not the supervisor's prerogative. All he should decide is whether he believes the chances of success on the job are good. Obvious emotional or personal problems— even though the supervisor does not know their cause or precisely what they are—mean trouble and should be avoided.

Verification of Education and Work History

All significant facts of an applicant's work history and education should be verified with former employers and schools before hiring. Employment dates should be checked out. The specific duties performed should be verified. Some evaluation of the man's performance and ability should be obtained from his immediate supervisor, if possible. If past employment was local, a telephone call may produce a more frank appraisal than a written inquiry would. If the job to be filled is a key one, long distance calls to out-of-town past employers are worthwhile. As a matter of fact, it is probably more important to check with out-of-town past employers than with others.

Some applicants who move from city to city may claim employment with several companies. Upon checking, the supervisor may find that the company never heard of the applicant, or that the company is nonexistent, or that the applicant's employment period was not of the duration claimed. One should be very wary of any applicant who is evasive about the exact addresses of past employers or the names of immediate supervisors. It is often desirable to ask the applicant directly, "Whom can we contact there about your employment?" It is also very suspicious if the applicant claims that everyone who knew him at his previous company has left or has died, or if he says that the company has gone out of business or has moved to an unknown city. This coincidence could occur once in a while, but, if a major part of an applicant's work history is unverifiable, there is strong reason to believe that it is fraudulent.

Whenever a job requires a particular educational background, the applicant's school record should be confirmed. He might be asked to obtain a transcript directly from the school. Licenses should be checked for any jobs that require licensing by state or local authorities. It is far better to take all necessary precautions before an individual is hired than to uncover a serious problem after he is on the job.

TRAINING NEW EMPLOYEES

Training starts as soon as selection is made. The first six months of employment are usually crucial. During this time, the employee will make up his mind whether he likes the work. And by the end of the period the supervisor should know what kind of contribution the employee may be expected to make.

Every hiring selection should be validated by a testing of actual performance. A new employee is similar to a new airplane in this respect. The plane may be perfect from an engineering standpoint, but it must be test-flown before its builders can give it final approval. Similarly, an employee may be perfectly suited to a job on the basis of his education, experience, and personal qualifications. But he must be tested on the job itself before an employer can be sure he is the right person. The selection tools that have been discussed are imperfect instruments. They are not foolproof. No matter how good the supervisor's judgment is, he will make a mistake in selection now and then. A supervisor would do well to consider his hiring selections as tentative decisions, subject to confirmation by on-the-job performance.

Some supervisors who fancy themselves good judges of men are defensive about their hiring choices. They cannot accept the fact that they may have made a mistake, even when confronted with overwhelming evidence that the man is not working out. They stubbornly refuse to see the new employee's shortcomings, and they may begin to cover up for him by doing part of his job or making decisions that he is supposed to make. This is certainly a self-defeating and totally unrealistic attitude. No one can choose exactly the right person for a job every time.

Orientation

Any new employee, regardless of his previous training and experience, feels strange and a little lost in a new organization. He does not know the people. He often cannot find his way to various departments or facilities. He does not know the policies of the company. And he is not sure of what is expected of him. The treatment he receives during the early days of his employment may condition his attitude toward the organization and toward the job.

On the first day of work, a new employee should be

informed in detail regarding personnel policies and practices and working conditions. He should be taken around and introduced to his co-workers and others with whom he will have contact. He should also meet some of the upper-level or executive personnel, especially those in direct line of authority over the unit. He should be shown the physical location of various departments and should be told something of the company or organization— what its products or services are, how it is organized, who the key executives are, how many people it employs, and other pertinent facts.

The duties of the job should then be discussed in detail with him. He should be told what will be expected of him. If the job has a specified training period, he should be told its duration. Supervisors often do not have time to train every new employee themselves, and they find it useful to assign a senior employee to this function. The supervisor should be sure, however, that the senior employee is really interested in training, that he understands the work, and that he knows *how* to train. (The supervisor should give him some coaching in the methods to use.)

A new employee should be put to work as soon as possible. Once the initial orientation has been accomplished, he should start performing productive work under whatever tutelage is necessary. It is undesirable to have a new employee spend the first week or so observing or reading before he tackles the job itself. Many new employees are given volumes of material to read. It is for the most part meaningless to them, since they cannot put it into any kind of context. They find it extremely boring and tedious. If the reading of manuals or other materials is necessary to the job training, it should be interspersed with the performance of actual duties.

Training Programs

The way a new employee is trained will depend upon the kind of work and the previous experience of the individual. Experienced managerial and professional employees do not need detailed instruction in the duties of their jobs. They do need to be informed about policies and objectives, about how things are done, about the problems they are likely to encounter, and where to go for materials or for help of various kinds. Many skilled and semiskilled jobs require only a similar general discussion of duties and responsibilities.

Most clerical jobs require specific instruction. They vary in their duties and they usually require that detailed procedures be followed. Manual and unskilled jobs normally require fairly detailed instruction.

When many jobs have similar duties and a number of new employees start at the same time, group training in a classroom setting is the most efficient method. Large department stores train groups of new sales clerks in those aspects of the sales jobs that are identical, such as preparing sales tickets and ordering and controlling merchandise, as well as in general sales policies and techniques. The same *vestibule* type of training can be successfully used to train groups of new factory workers, telephone repairmen, industrial salesmen, nurses' aides, police officers, and many other occupations. If employees are hired one at a time and the jobs vary substantially in duties, individual training on the job is necessary.

Whether the training is done individually or in groups, it should proceed by a definite plan. Trainees in classes should not sit for hours or days listening to speakers or watching demonstrations, any more than a new employee who is being trained individually should spend hours or days observing work or reading materials. In either case, the employees should be involved directly in the work as soon as possible.

The job instructor training program (part of the training-within-industry series developed during World War II) had a simplified four-step formula for training: (1) Explain the task to the employee, (2) demonstrate it to him, (3) have him do it, and (4) follow up and check his results. This formula is still valid today. Work should be broken up into suitable learning units. A new employee should be told briefly the total responsibility and scope of a job so that he will see the overall picture, but he should be taught duties one at a time in manageable chunks. Each one should first be explained and demonstrated to him. Then he should perform the duty while the trainer observes him and intervenes when he makes mistakes or misses details.

It is of utmost importance that an employee understand *why* a certain duty is being performed. It is very hard to learn something that is not understandable. For this reason, considerable thought should be given to the way the work is divided up into learning units. It should not be broken up so much that the duty makes no sense to the employee. It should have a logical beginning and an end. However, it should not be so complex or so lengthy that he has to remember voluminous instructions before he has a chance to try performing it.

Classroom instruction should contain a similar mixture of instruction, demonstration, trial or practice, and follow-up and evaluation. Straight lecture is being used less and less as a teaching method. Most educators believe that the active participation of the trainee through practice, discussion, or role playing is necessary to learning.

If anyone other than the supervisor trains new employees, the supervisor should follow up frequently and should check on each employee's progress by talking to both the trainer and the employee.

A supervisor's responsibility for training does not end when an employee has learned the duties of his job and is performing them proficiently. He should continue to develop his employees by giving them increasing responsibility and more difficult work. Large organizations often have central facilities for teaching employees new skills. In a small- or medium-size organization, the supervisor must undertake this training himself. He should recognize employees who have the interest and intelligence to learn new skills, and, if he has jobs that require the skills in question, he should help them as much as he can. He should encourage employees to develop themselves by enrolling in night classes to learn new skills or to gain further education.

Much training is designed to keep employees abreast of current developments in their field or to broaden their outlook and understanding. Training never ends for professional and managerial employees because of rapid changes in technology and advances in knowledge and research. A supervisor can help keep his staff on their toes and motivated by holding periodic seminars or workshops on new developments in the field, new techniques, new ideas, or new policies. This kind of training is especially desirable when employees are stationed in outlying areas. These employees should be brought into the headquarters office at regular intervals for refresher training sessions and discussions.

Problems of Hiring and Training the Underprivileged

Supervisors are being called upon more and more to hire school dropouts, individuals from deprived backgrounds, or the hard-core unemployed who have completed special training programs. These employees vary greatly in motivation, native intelligence, and aptitudes. Some may adapt readily to the work situation and perform at about the same level as other new workers, while some may require a great deal of personal attention from the supervisor.

Every effort should be made to assess the employees' knowledge, motivation, and aptitudes before hiring and to place them on jobs in which they have the best chance of success. For example, a girl who is very deficient in language skills should not be placed on a trainee secretarial or stenographic job or a job dealing with the public. She would either fail or require an inordinate amount of training and basic education before she could perform at an acceptable level. On the other hand, she might perform quite well as an operator of simple duplicating machines or in work that required motor skills or manual dexterity.

A chance to succeed at an early date is very important psychologically to employees with a background of failure or lack of achievement. If they must go through a very long training period before they can learn a job or see any signs of progress, they might well become discouraged and may give up completely. It is far better to place them initially on jobs that they can learn fairly quickly. Then, after they have adjusted to the work environment and have demonstrated their ability to handle more difficult work, they may be advanced to other jobs.

New employees who have become accustomed to lives that are completely unregulated and undisciplined may have extreme difficulty in conforming to office rules and practices, such as getting to work on time or coming to work every day. They may find it nearly impossible to stick to a job for an eight-hour stretch. The supervisor will usually have to devote a large amount of time and attention to these employees. He should help them develop good work habits and should try to instill in them a sense of responsibility. He needs to have a great deal of patience, but at the same time he must be quite firm in insisting that the employees conform. He should require them to adhere to the same policies as other employees. He should not be more lenient with them, nor should he grant them privileges that other employees do not have. When minority group individuals are hired, supervisors sometimes feel constrained to "bend over backwards" and give them preferential treatment. This is entirely wrong. They should be treated as individuals in the same manner as all other employees. The supervisor's prime objective should be to develop the employees into productive workers who contribute to the organization. He should not consider his efforts to be in the area of social service or welfare.

The supervisor may find that employees from underprivileged backgrounds lack rudimentary knowledge that is commonly taken for granted. For example, one school dropout who was hired as a clerical trainee was unable to tell the time of day, to count, or to add and subtract simple numbers.

Newly employed individuals from substandard backgrounds will generally adopt the behavior patterns and attitudes of the experienced employees with whom they work. It is important, therefore, that they be placed with employees who are capable and productive and who are positively motivated. The work itself should be structured and orderly. These employees should never be placed in a group whose members are poor performers or disgruntled and unhappy, or where the work is confused and unsystematic or too fluid. They should not be placed in a group that consists largely of individuals of like backgrounds. They will have no example to follow and will merely learn and reinforce each other's bad habits.

10

Living with
Regulations and Contracts

SUPERVISION IS NOT AN ISLAND UNTO IT-
self. No superior has unrestricted freedom to manage
his unit or direct his employees any way he sees fit. He
is guided in his various actions by policies established by
top management. He is governed by federal and state
laws on working hours, minimum wages, overtime pay,
and the like. Large private companies or organizations
frequently have formal personnel policies covering job
evaluation and rates of pay, working hours, overtime,
holidays, vacations, and sick leave, as well as policies
regarding employment, promotion, and discharge.

Nevertheless, particular responsibilities are placed on

supervisors when their employees are covered by civil service regulations or by a union contract. These regulations and contract provisions are far more detailed and legalistic than are the personnel policies of most private organizations. Moreover, they bring a third party—the civil service agency or the union—into the supervisor-employee relationship.

Civil Service Regulations

Civil service laws and regulations historically were established to remove the employment of government workers from the realm of political patronage or the "spoils system." Regulations covering the employment relationship were likewise intended to prevent favoritism and to protect employees against arbitrary treatment or discharge by politically motivated bosses.

Many civil service systems have now become anachronisms, dated in purpose and philosophy and out of tune with modern concepts of personnel management. By permitting employees innumerable channels of appeal, they frequently obstruct management, waste time, and encourage employees to pursue causes that have little merit. Nonetheless, a supervisor in a civil service system must live with these regulations. He must be familiar with them and understand how they affect his relations with his employees.

Many civil service supervisors consider themselves to be much more restricted than they in fact are. They erroneously assume that they cannot require employees to do certain tasks, they cannot demand superior performance, or they cannot discharge employees no matter what the provocation. This is not true, although there are numerous examples in any civil service system of employees being permitted to perform as if it were true. Perhaps the greatest weakness of all in the system is the passive, uninterested attitude that it has fostered among supervisors and employees alike.

Supervisors should understand that civil service regulations merely establish a framework and procedures for governing their relation with their employees. They prohibit a superior from hiring just anyone he wants. Individuals hired must have qualified under the established examination process, and they must have received a score high enough to place them near the top of a register of eligibles. (Most systems require that the individual hired be among the top three or five on the list of eligibles.) The purpose of this requirement is twofold. First, it is intended to give every citizen the same opportunity for public employment by requiring that every applicant be rated by the same examining procedure. Second, it is intended to insure that only well-qualified individuals be brought into the public service.

Once a person has been hired, the civil service regulations normally apply to such items as job classification and pay, hours of work, vacation, sick leave, holidays, and retirement provisions. Regulations usually provide for some form of internal promotion system. Some civil service plans require that candidates for promotion go through an examining process similar to that for initial employment and that selection be made from candidates who place among the top three or five on the promotion list.

Discharges are not prohibited, as many supervisors believe. Most systems do prohibit discharges without notice (except on grounds of moral turpitude or serious offenses), and they prohibit discharges that are made arbitrarily without supporting reasons. Most systems also provide a procedural mechanism for discharging employees, including written warnings specifying the charges, allowance of a certain amount of time for improvement, and discharge notice if the improvement is not forthcoming.

Virtually all systems provide for a probationary period during which a new employee must demonstrate his fitness for a job in order to be retained. The period usually lasts six months to a year. It is during this stage that the supervisor should spend a great deal of time with the new employee, training him and evaluating his performance. An employee who is unable to perform the work satisfactorily after adequate training should not be retained past the probationary period.

Employees do have appeal rights. They may appeal supervisory actions to higher levels of management or to the central civil service agency.

Within the civil service provisions, the supervisor has a broad area of freedom to plan and organize the work, to assign duties, to establish controls over the work, to maintain high standards of performance, to train and develop employees, and to maintain discipline and decorum in the work unit. He should carry out his responsibilities fully and with confidence in his ability as a supervisor. He should establish rapport with his employees and stimulate them to continued improvement of performance. If he has to take an action that will not sit well with an employee, he should be sure of his ground, be prepared to support his actions with documented facts if necessary, and then proceed to act regardless of whether he expects the employee to appeal his action.

Many performance problems under civil service develop because supervisors have not assumed their responsibilities. They may not have trained the employee adequately. They may not have demanded a high level of performance. They may have permitted unsatisfactory employees to remain on the payroll past the probationary period. They may have tolerated innumerable violations of performance or discipline, such as repeated absences or tardiness. A lax atmosphere of this kind is conducive to poor performance. An employee who has gotten by with inadequate performance for a long time will naturally object and appeal if the supervisor suddenly decides to correct the situation by disciplining him.

Union Contracts

The effect of a union contract on the supervisory relationship is somewhat similar to that of civil service regulations, although the language and specific provisions are often quite different. One major difference is that civil service systems usually require that promotions be based on merit, while union contracts sometimes provide a strict seniority basis for promotions. Many aspects of the contractual relationship are defined in legalistic language. Alleged violations or disputes over interpretation of the contract provisions are subject to formal grievance procedures, whose outcome is determined by someone other than the supervisor. A third party—the union—enters the supervisor-employee relationship.

A union contract may be more difficult to administer than civil service regulations. Contract provisions are frequently very technical, particularly with respect to seniority provisions and grievance procedures. The union contract is often more restrictive on the supervisor. The union is ever present because of the system of shop stewards generally in use. It is always available to help employees prepare grievances or to challenge an action of a supervisor that might violate the contract. Yet within the contract provisions the supervisor has a large area of responsibility and freedom in supervising employees. He has more freedom in hiring under the union contract than under civil service, although contracts often require that anyone hired must join the union. He may be restricted in making promotions if the contract includes a strict seniority clause.

It certainly behooves a supervisor to know and understand the contract in its entirety; he should be thoroughly conversant with those provisions that directly affect the way he performs his job. The parts of a contract most relevant to him are those pertaining to jobs covered by the agreement, union security, rights of management, grievance procedures, job classifications and rates of pay, promotions, demotions, transfers, layoffs, discharges, vacation pay and scheduling of vacations, sick leave, distribution of overtime, holidays, leaves of absence and maternity leave, and jury duty. It is also helpful if the supervisor has some understanding of the prevailing philosophy of labor unions and of the most likely differences in points of view between the union and management.

Contract Coverage and Union Security

Most labor contracts specify what jobs are covered by the contract and what jobs are excluded. The most common exclusions are supervisory jobs and jobs whose duties place them in a confidential relationship with management. The latter exclusion might apply to secretaries of top executives, personnel and accounting department employees, and, frequently, guards and watchmen.

Union security provisions which establish the requirements for union membership are of four kinds: open shop, agency shop, union shop and modifications of it, and maintenance of membership. Under an open shop provision, the union represents for collective bargaining purposes all employees in the jobs covered by the contract, but no employee is required to join the union as a condition of employment. Under an agency shop, no one is required to join the union, but all employees covered by the agreement are required to pay an amount of money equivalent to regular union dues and initiation fees as a condition of employment. Under the union shop, all persons employed in jobs covered by the contract on its effective date and all persons subsequently hired are required to join the union and to maintain their membership in good standing. A modified union shop may exempt from the membership requirement those individuals employed on the effective date of the contract, while requiring anyone subsequently hired to join the union. Union shop clauses often require the employer to notify the union of job vacancies so that the union might supply candidates. However, the employer may also use other recruiting sources, and he is not required to select the applicant sent by the union. Maintenance-of-membership clauses provide that all persons covered by the contract who are employed on its effective date are required to join the union and to maintain their membership in good standing. Persons subsequently hired are not required to join. The closed shop, which provided that an employer hire only union members referred by union hiring halls, was outlawed by the Labor-Management Relations Act of 1947 (the Taft-Hartley Act). The union shop, or a modified version of it, is the union security provision most commonly found in contracts.

Union security clauses that require employees to join the union may be a source of friction between supervisors and the union. If the employee refuses to join, the union may request that he be terminated and the employer is required to do so. Some contracts stipulate that the union must be in a position to supply the employer with an acceptable replacement before it demands that an employee be terminated for nonmembership in the union. But many contracts contain no such provision, in which case the employer is obligated to terminate the employee. When interviewing for jobs covered by a contract that contains a union shop clause, the supervisor should be sure that the individuals hired understand the requirements for joining the union.

All contracts contain a clause prohibiting discrimination against employees for joining the union or for engaging in union activity. Most contracts now also prohibit discrimination against any employee because of race, color, creed, or national origin. The nondiscrimination clause is often used as a basis for grievances, particularly in cases where the complaint would otherwise be inadmissible under the grievance procedure. For example, a contract may exclude from the grievance procedure discharges for repeated failure after due warning to meet normally expected performance standards. Yet, if an employee is discharged, he may file a grievance claiming that the true reason for his discharge was not his failure to meet performance standards but the fact that he was an active member of the union. Or he may claim discrimination because of his race, religion, or national origin.

Rights of Management and Grievance Procedures

Some contracts set forth certain rights reserved to management. These usually are the rights to direct the workforce, to control production, to determine the size of the workforce, to hire, promote, and discharge employees, to establish shifts and working hours, and to introduce new machinery or equipment.

Some contracts specifically limit these prerogatives by providing for joint union-management decision. For example, a contract may require prior consultation with the union before new machinery or equipment is introduced, and it may require mutual agreement by union and management on jobs and rates of pay resulting from the use of the new machinery. Management may be prohibited from laying off employees without the prior consent of the union. Seniority provisions often limit management's right to promote or demote. Subcontracting work is often a controversial issue. Some contracts give management an unrestricted right in this respect, while others may require bargaining with the union on any subcontracting decisions that may result in a decrease of jobs.

In the absence of a clause setting forth management rights, it is presupposed that management has all rights that are not abridged by the terms of the agreement or by specific laws. Whether stated in the contract or not, management's rights are rarely absolute, since virtually any decision affecting the rights or working conditions of employees is subject to the grievance procedure. Management decisions regarding manufacturing processes, types of products or services to be marketed, sales strategies, and selling prices or profit margins are virtually always excluded from the grievance procedure and from the collective bargaining process as well.

Grievance machinery is usually described in detail. Contracts specify the successive levels of management to which the grievance may be presented, as well as the union representation available to the employee at each step. The grievance procedure normally culminates in the joint selection of an impartial arbitrator or panel of arbitrators who will render a binding decision in disputes that cannot be resolved at lower levels.

The kinds of complaints that are admissible under the grievance procedure are frequently defined. Most often, they are complaints or disputes regarding the meaning and application of the provisions of the contract. Proposed changes in the terms of the agreement (for example, changes in the contract pay rates, vacation, and sick pay) are not admissible under the grievance machinery. Rather, they are subjects for collective bargaining when the contract expires.

As a practical matter, most personnel actions by the supervisor are subject to the grievance procedure. If he fails to promote a particular employee, or if he transfers, lays off, discharges, or changes the work assignment of an employee, violation of some provision of the contract can usually be claimed. If not, the employee may often use the nondiscrimination clause as a basis for a grievance. Even if a particular complaint may not be admissible under the formal grievance machinery, it may be the subject of informal discussions between union representatives and management. If it is not resolved, it may become a festering sore between the two parties. And it will very likely become a union demand at the next round of contract negotiations.

Job Classifications and Rates of Pay

Contracts normally provide for a series of job classifications with a rate of pay for each. In some agreements the various classifications are clearly defined, while in others they may consist merely of a series of job titles. An employee's dissatisfaction with the classification of his job is nearly always admissible under the grievance procedure, and many disputes can arise from this part of the contract.

Awkward administrative problems can result from situations where there are overlapping classifications, or where employees perform some duties for a portion of their time that fall into a higher classification, or where an employee performs the duties of a higher classification for a single day during an emergency. At the time of contract negotiations, management should insist on including a simple mechanism for handling these assorted situations. It is incumbent upon the supervisors who are most familiar with the problems to bring them to the attention of higher-level management.

Job classifications may also create jurisdictional disputes between two or more crafts working on the same job, since one union may claim the right to perform work that is being done by another craft union.

Role of Seniority

Perhaps on no other issue is there such a wide divergence of views between management and unions as there is on seniority. At the insistence of the union, many contracts provide that promotions shall be made on a strict seniority basis. The employee who has worked for the company the longest shall be the one promoted, even if he is less capable than some other employee. Contracts with such a promotion clause often provide for the posting of job vacancy notices on bulletin boards so that employees may bid on them. A provision of this kind denies supervisors the right to make individual judgments about their employees and to reward those who contribute the most. A strict seniority clause, however, will often be tempered by a proviso that the employee shall be fully qualified to perform the job to which he is promoted.

The seniority rule often applies to layoffs: The worker with the least seniority shall be laid off first, and the worker with the highest seniority shall be the first recalled to work. Contracts often require that employees be given preference of vacation dates in accordance with their seniority.

Sometimes the seniority rule on promotions is relaxed by providing that, if two or more employees have approximately equal qualifications, the one with the greatest seniority shall be chosen. Many grievances can result from a clause of this kind. It is often quite difficult to show that one employee has greater qualifications than another. They may have very much the same training and experience, but one may be brighter, more alert, or a harder worker. Unless the supervisor has some objective means of measuring performance, such as production figures, he may find it difficult to support his reasons for selecting the employee with the lower seniority.

A strict seniority provision makes it mandatory that supervisors be selective in hiring, that they train their employees, and that they make continuous, objective evaluations of performance and keep written records of their evaluations. Nearly all contracts provide for an initial probationary period of varying lengths of time. The employee frequently does not earn seniority rights during the probationary period, and a discharge for poor performance during that period is often not admissible under the grievance procedure.

Discharges

Seniority plays an important, often covert role in grievances over discharges. Most contracts state that employees may be discharged for just cause or for repeated failure after due warning to meet performance standards. The interpretation of just cause or poor performance can provoke a great deal of controversy.

If an employee commits a serious breach of conduct—for example, stealing tools or money, falsifying his time card or other official records, or being drunk on the job—he is always subject to immediate dismissal. It would be very unusual for a union to file a grievance in a discharge of this kind. If a grievance were filed, it would not get very far.

Discharges for poor performance, however, are something else entirely. A supervisor is always in a weak position when he discharges a long-service employee for poor performance. The question is invariably asked, "How is it that the employee was satisfactory for all these years and now all of a sudden is no good?" Of course, the employee's performance may have deteriorated. Or perhaps a new supervisor refuses to tolerate the poor performance that his predecessor accepted. If the discharge is justified, a supervisor should not shrink from it because the employee has high seniority. He should be careful, however, to document thoroughly the instances of poor performance in a written warning notice to the employee. The warning should give the employee a specified time in which to improve his performance, and it should state unequivocally just what improvement is required. If performance continues below the acceptable level at the end of the warning period, the employee should be discharged.

Timing is very important in a discharge for poor performance. One supervisor had been very dissatisfied for a long time with an employee's performance but had done nothing about it. Then the employee became ill and was off from work for three weeks. During his absence the supervisor hired a replacement, and he discharged the employee immediately upon his return to work from his illness. Naturally the employee filed a grievance, claiming that he was discharged because he was sick.

Provisions Regarding Other Working Conditions

Contracts generally contain specific stipulations regarding the amount of paid vacation and sick leave earned, the method of paying for it in various situations, the number of paid holidays, and the pay rates when an employee works on a holiday. They often specify that an employee may not be transferred to another kind of work without his consent. They may provide for leaves of absence without pay under certain circumstances, and they usually provide for maternity leave. They frequently require that overtime be distributed equally among employees, and they always specify the rates of overtime pay.

The Union Point of View

Seniority and union security are two principles to which many unions attach great importance. Several reasons underlie the emphasis on seniority. Basically, union representatives have a deep distrust of the merit principle. They do not have confidence in the ability of supervisors to make objective and fair evaluations of subordinates. Rather, they believe most evaluations are grossly distorted by personal favoritism and bias. They think the unrestricted freedom to promote or to discharge gives supervisors far too much power over the lives of employees. Union representatives undoubtedly have acquired this skepticism in part from experiences with supervisors who were less than adequate.

Moreover, a strict seniority system makes the life of a union representative far easier. Unions have an obligation to represent employees who are dissatisfied with the treatment accorded them. The union representatives like to devote their time and effort to handling grievances that they can win, because winning a fair number of cases is essential if employee confidence and support are to be maintained. Probably no situation is harder to present or to win than the case of an employee who was not selected for promotion under a merit system. It is extremely difficult to prove that another employee was better qualified than the individual selected—unless, of course, the person selected was so unqualified that any reasonable person would recognize the fact.

Qualifications are hardly ever exactly equal. One person has a little more of this experience and training, while someone else has a little more of that experience and training or some other special abilities. A supervisor can always claim that the person he selected had precisely the right combination of talents and background that the job needed, while the individual not selected lacked some particular thing. By contrast, a seniority system is very clear-cut and easy to enforce. It makes employees happy because they know they will be promoted if they remain with the organization long enough. They are grateful for the job the union is doing for them.

Unions are *institutions* that wish to perpetuate themselves. They also are egalitarian. Each member who keeps up his dues is as good as any other member. The union has a totally different set of criteria for measuring value from that used by the supervisor. The individual most valuable to the union is the person who keeps up his dues, who takes an active part in union affairs by serving as a shop steward or in some other capacity, and who actively promotes membership in the union. This same person may or may not be the best employee so far as his supervisor is concerned. The supervisor may think he is more interested in the union than he is in his job. Or he may have a distrustful attitude that irritates the supervisor. The employee's value to his supervisor is immaterial to the union as an institution, so long as the employee does not lose his job through discharge.

A union attaches great importance to union security provisions in contracts because of its strong desire to perpetuate itself as an institution. At the time a contract is signed, the union is supposed to represent a majority of employees in the bargaining unit. It may demonstrate this fact either by winning a representation election or by showing that a majority of employees are its members. It does not want to jeopardize its status by having members drop out. It does not want management to challenge its majority representation when the contract is up for renegotiation. Moreover, the regular receipt of dues is essential to keep the union going. From the union point of view, therefore, all employees who are served by the union should be required to join and to maintain their membership in good standing. Unions argue this point on grounds of fairness or ethics. They say that everyone who benefits from the union should pay his fair share of the costs; it is unfair for some employees to be "free loaders." The desire to maintain the union as a strong and viable institution, however, is a primary reason for the concern with union security.

Why Employees Join Unions

Supervisors sometimes find it difficult to understand why their employees want to join a union or want to have the union represent them. They may be offended when employees go to their union representative instead of to their supervisor with a problem. On occasion, a supervisor may discuss a change in duties with an employee and leave the interview in the belief that the employee is perfectly happy with the change. The next thing he knows, the shop steward has presented him with a grievance filed by the employee.

There are many different reasons why employees want to be represented by a union. Each individual may have his own reasons. Economic considerations are no doubt the primary cause for a union's successful organization of a group of employees. The employees believe they will receive higher pay and better fringe benefits and working conditions if they are represented by a union. Some individual employees who lack the ability and drive to advance on their own merits may believe they can achieve more success and status by actively promoting a union.

Supervisory relationships and the personnel policies of the organization have a great deal to do with the success of a union's organizing drive. Many union contracts have been built on the foundation of an accumulation of unresolved employee grievances over erratic management policies and unfair supervisory practices. Employees believe they will receive fairer treatment and have a better chance for promotion if they are supported by the bargaining power of a strong union.

Supervisors often think they have better communications with their employees than they actually have. The communications may all be one way. They may tell the employees what they want, but they never hear or perceive what the employees think or feel. The employees may be seething with hostility, but their attitudes fail to penetrate the wall of indifference surrounding the supervisor.

We might also speculate on how much union success is due to the classical organization structure that has been decried so vehemently by the behavioral scientists. In the past few years, there has been a significant increase in the union activity and the militancy of Federal Government employees. This is an interesting phenomenon when pay, fringe benefits, and most working conditions are excluded from the area of collective bargaining and when employees are protected by civil service regulations. This development may signify a ground swell of reaction against the monotony that characterizes many government jobs, overdefined as they are and divested of interest and responsibility. Or it may be a reaction against the bureaucratic organization structure, with its layers upon layers of authority and the inevitable communication barriers between the bottom of the pyramid and the top.

The Supervisor's Obligations

A supervisor has three main obligations when his subordinates are covered by a union contract. In the first place, he should know and understand the provisions of the contract. If some of its terms are unclear to him, he should consult with the management official who negotiated it. He should administer the contract fairly and in good faith. He should also deal with union representatives openly and frankly. He should recognize their right to inquire about personnel actions that he has taken. He may find that the union representatives can be helpful to him by facilitating communications with employees or by helping interpret plans and policies to them. He should express his own ideas and objectives to the union representatives and make them acquainted with the problems he faces. He should discuss with them impending changes that are likely to disturb employees.

A second major obligation the supervisor has is to exercise leadership and authority over his unit. Occasionally, a supervisor will abdicate his role when confronted with a union contract. He mistakenly believes he no longer has power to supervise employees or to maintain high standards of performance. Some supervisors have gone so far as to say they cannot discharge an unsatisfactory employee who is a member of the union. It would be hard to imagine a union contract that contained any such provision.

A supervisor should not read into a contract restrictions that are not there. Union representatives have sometimes assumed a position of power in organizations far beyond anything the contract terms have given them. They exercise virtual veto power over basic management decisions and, in effect, serve as co-managers. This unhealthy state is invariably the fault of weak and unsophisticated managers and supervisors who are afraid to assert their own rights. A supervisor should have confidence in his ability to manage his unit. He should be sure of his ground; then he should make decisions and stick to them.

Finally, the supervisor has an obligation to communicate to higher levels of management problems he has encountered in working with the contract. He should propose changes that he thinks management should request at the next round of negotiations. Too often, management makes few demands of its own and merely waits to respond to the demands of the union. Contracts negotiated in this atmosphere can be very one-sided. Moreover, the management official who negotiates the contract often has had no firsthand experience with the day-to-day operation of the contract. He may agree to provisions that become monstrous problems in administration. Supervisors are the individuals in any organization who have the most experience with union contracts. They should have a voice in proposing changes in the terms of the agreement.

II

Technology and Change

$\mathcal{M}$ANY SUPERVISORS IN TODAY'S RAPIDLY changing world must face the prospect of having the work under them change dramatically in volume or in kind or even be eliminated altogether. Technological advances over the past 15 years have been revolutionary. Many jobs have completely disappeared and in their place have come new jobs requiring far different skills and training.

In former years, unskilled and uneducated people could work as elevator operators. To a large extent, these jobs have now been eliminated and the employees displaced by automatic, self-service elevators. A tremendous number of clerical and routine accounting jobs have ceased to exist, and the work has been transferred to the computer. Not so many years ago, a Comptometer operator was a well-paid, semiskilled person. Today, one never even hears the term. She has long since been replaced by a computer. Many telephone operators have been displaced by direct dialing. Manual material handlers and construction laborers have been displaced by power machinery. Many print shop jobs have been eliminated by automatic typesetting equipment. Railroad jobs have been displaced by automatic devices of various kinds. The automated factory assembly line has replaced many semi-skilled jobs.

The result of this technological revolution has not been mass unemployment, as many had feared. The technology itself has created a vast army of new jobs in such fields as computers or among power machinery operators. The technology has contributed to a growing and expanding economy. When the first computers were introduced into banks, there was widespread fear of tremendous hardship resulting from the unemployment of bank clerks. On the contrary, the rapid expansion of banks since the early part of the 1950's has created the need for many additional clerical employees, particularly tellers.

The new jobs created by technology have been different. They have required new skills and often different aptitudes. The bank teller must have different attributes from the clerk who posted accounts. Skills and aptitudes required for the various computer jobs, such as programmer or systems analyst or computer operator, are far different from those required by an accounting clerk. The skills and training required for the operation of heavy power machinery for material handling or earth moving are not even comparable to those required of a laborer, whose most essential quality was physical strength and endurance.

Technological advances have not been limited to the introduction of automatic or power-driven equipment.

240 • DYNAMIC SUPERVISION

There have been vast changes in methods of marketing and distribution. Retail selling has moved more and more in the direction of self-service. The trend began with grocery stores and has rapidly extended to large drug and variety stores. Large department stores are increasingly adopting self-service methods in many of their departments.

Marketing and distribution methods at the manufacturing or wholesale stage have had an impact at the retail or user level. The introduction of economical disposable supplies of all kinds has eliminated routine, unskilled jobs in hospitals. Employees formerly engaged in cleaning and sterilizing needles, syringes, rubber gloves, and other kinds of supplies or equipment have been displaced by the use of a vast array of disposable goods. The use of precut meats and prepackaged or frozen foods and vegetables has eliminated butchering and food-preparation jobs in restaurants. New products and new methods are continually being developed that prove to be economical as labor savers.

All of these technological improvements have benefited the nation's economy and the individual organizations taking advantage of them. And in the long run they have produced an increase in jobs. Nevertheless, they have created serious dislocations for the individual employees affected. The introduction of a computer to replace a group of clerks is a distressing experience to the employees concerned. If the employees know that the computer will do the work of 25 clerks now employed, they will not be comforted when told that in the long run the expansion of the industry will produce many new jobs or that within the next five years the company is expected to open up new offices and branches, many of which will be in outlying areas. The only thing the employees are concerned with is what they will do now, if their jobs are eliminated. Some may be older employees who dread the thought of having to learn new skills or having to adjust to a new job or to new co-workers. Others may have family responsibilities that preclude their accepting jobs in out-of-town locations or even in other parts of the same town.

The supervisor is the focal point for all of the problems, anxieties, and disruptions created by technological change. He is responsible to management for successfully introducing the change and for making it work. At the same time, he must deal with the anxieties and emotions of the employees who will be dislocated. He must decide how and when he will tell them of the impending change and what assurances, if any, he can give them about their continued employment. He must decide what to do about employees whose jobs surely will be eliminated. Does he just terminate them? Does he try to retrain them for other jobs in the organization? Does he try to help them find other jobs in the community? He must decide how to keep them from becoming panic-stricken and immediately trying to find other jobs, so that he will be short-staffed and unable to keep the work current before the change is introduced. His task is made doubly difficult because he is often not sure of what will happen to his own job, and he has many of the same anxieties as his employees.

Nontechnological Change

Technological innovation is usually the most dramatic change affecting jobs, simply because it often results in revolutionary new methods of performing work and because it often displaces large numbers of employees. It is not, however, the only change that affects jobs or employees or that requires great skill in handling on the part of the supervisor.

Management decisions of various kinds can have effects just as serious. The decision to centralize the purchasing function or the warehouse operations, for example, will most probably displace a number of jobs, as will decisions to curtail production, to discontinue a particular service, or to eliminate or combine various functions or organizational units. A retrenchment owing to economic factors can have substantial effect on jobs and on employees. A company that has many defense contracts will have to eliminate jobs if there is a substantial reduction in defense spending or if it loses its contracts. A decline in sales or in demand for a service, whatever the cause, usually results in a contraction of jobs. Company mergers nearly always create job dislocations.

The supervisor himself may deliberately create the dislocation of certain jobs by improving and streamlining work methods. He might see that a particular function is no longer worthwhile and should be discontinued. He might decide that the work could be done more efficiently if two jobs were combined. Organizational and procedural change of many kinds have a major influence on jobs and employees.

In a dynamic economy, the potential for change is almost unlimited. Nor is this potential confined to business and industry. Nonprofit organizations of various kinds undergo continuing change. Several hospitals may merge individual departments, such as obstetrics, for greater economy or better utilization of beds; they may even merge in their entirety. Government agencies may contract their employment sharply under the pressure of budget cuts or the curtailment of programs, or they may undergo internal organizational changes that result in a different mix of jobs.

Not all changes result in the elimination of jobs, of course. Some changes merely require that employees use different methods or new procedures which can be readily learned. Other changes require that jobs be restructured and that employees take on totally different duties and learn new skills. Supervisors often find it as hard to introduce fairly minor changes in work methods as they do to introduce sweeping changes that have far reaching effects on jobs and duties.

Understanding Reasons for Resistance

Resistance to change is a commonly used phrase. It is often used as an epithet by managers and supervisors to express their frustration in getting employees to accept change willingly. There is no single approach that a supervisor should take in handling job changes, whether they are minor or drastic. Each situation is different, and often the reasons for the employees' resistance are different.

The first step a supervisor should take in effecting change is to understand the feelings of his employees. Everyone resists change when it is seen as a threat to his livelihood, to his career, to his status, or to his comfortable social relationships and work patterns. Everyone resists change when he cannot quite predict what its outcome or its effect on him will be; when he does not understand it; when he is unable to see any rational reason for it. Once the supervisor identifies the main reason for the employee's resistance, he is better able to deal with it constructively. The following cases are typical of different kinds of change and the ways a supervisor might handle them.

Gradual job reduction. An organization decided to convert gradually all of its accounting records to the computer. Operations would be changed over one at a time. The supervisor would be sure that each one was working smoothly before beginning the conversion of another operation. The payroll function was to be the first converted. After the new system was working, the job of payroll clerk would be eliminated. The organization's policy was that no one would be terminated; all displaced employees would be absorbed in other jobs in different parts of the organization. The complete conversion of accounting was expected to take a year. Normal turnover was expected to take care of many of the jobs displaced by the computer. Any employees remaining in the department at the end of the conversion period would be transferred to the expanding market research department, where the work would be statistical and analytical and would require little retraining.

The supervisor talked to the entire group of accounting employees and explained the plan for gradually converting the records to the computer. He assured them that no one would lose his job, that upon completion of the conversion, they would be reassigned to other jobs in the organization. He did not tell them specifically about the market research department. He talked in more detail to the payroll clerk and told her that he needed her help in making the conversion. He said that after the payroll had been changed over, he wanted to run duplicate payrolls two or three times to make sure the computer system was working accurately. He reassured her that there was plenty of other work in the accounting department for her to do and that after the entire conversion had been completed, she would be reassigned to another job in the organization.

Although the payroll clerk had little to say at the time, the supervisor could see later that she strongly resisted the conversion of her job to the computer. She threw up various roadblocks and insisted that she would have to check all work coming from the computer to make sure no mistakes were made. The supervisor could not understand the reason for her resistance and talked to her again. He reassured her that she would not lose her job but would be reassigned somewhere else in the organization.

The supervisor mistakenly believed that employees were only concerned about economic loss when their jobs were abolished. He thought he could overcome the payroll clerk's resistance to the change by repeatedly reassuring her that she would have another job in the organization. Employees are often just as disturbed over the threat to their established work patterns and relationships as they are over the threat they may lose their means of livelihood. The payroll clerk no doubt knew and understood her job thoroughly. She was comfortable in it. She had confidence in her ability to do it. She liked the interpersonal relationships that the job involved. Now suddenly she was to be uprooted from her own job and put on some other kind of work. She pictured herself being assigned to do odd jobs in the accounting department and all of the details that no one else wanted to do. She resented this prospect because she thought it was demeaning to her status and ability. Then she began to think about what regular job she might be transferred to. The supervisor had always had trouble keeping the job of accounts payable clerk filled. No one liked the amount of detail on it; she had filled in there once and disliked it too. She began to believe that she knew exactly what was in the supervisor's mind. As soon as the payroll job was abolished, he would offer her the accounts payable job and she would have to take it or quit. The more she thought about her situation, the more hostility she felt toward the supervisor for the way he was treating her.

Many employees intensely dislike ambiguity in their work. They want to know where they stand and what they will be doing tomorrow and the next day. The supervisor could have handled this case better by discussing another permanent job with the payroll clerk immediately. If there was a job in the market research department, it might have been better to transfer her to it immediately upon the successful conversion of the payroll to the computer. At any rate, the proposed job should have been discussed with her and she should have had an opportunity to interview the market research supervisor. She might have resisted giving up the payroll job in any event, but she undoubtedly would have accepted the change more cheerfully if she had known she would be moving on to a definite and interesting new job.

A technological change that drags on for a long period of time is difficult for everyone concerned. Duties become confused and employees work in a continual state of indefiniteness. During the year of conversion, part of the accounting work would have been on the computer and part of it would not. It would have been a trying time, especially when the employees knew that ultimately their jobs would be eliminated. It would have been difficult for the supervisor to keep up their interest. Once a decision has been made to introduce a technological change of a sweeping nature, it is better to do it as quickly as possible and get it over with. The dislocations that will result will at least be brief, and then concentrated efforts can be made to get the new system working smoothly.

Immediate job reduction. A supervisor has an entirely different problem when a technological innovation results in an immediate elimination of jobs. The manager of a variety chain store employing 25 sales clerks received a telegram from the controller at the headquarters office in another city informing him that management had decided to convert all of its stores to self-service because of reduced profit margins. The effective date for the change was to be in 30 days, and all excess sales jobs were to be eliminated by that time. All employees affected by the job reduction would be given two weeks' separation pay. The telegram requested the manager to develop a plan for making the conversion and to telephone the controller, letting him know how many sales jobs would be abolished.

The manager may have had some inkling that this change was about to be made, or he may not have. In any event, he is faced with a time deadline for planning and putting the conversion into effect. The decisions he must now make are: How many cashier stands and how many cashiers will be needed? What new equipment and what changes in physical layout of the store will be required? Which of the 25 clerks should be retained as cashiers and which ones should be terminated? When and how should the news be broken to the employees?

After analyzing his daily sales records, he decides to retain five clerks to be trained as cashiers. As soon as he telephones the controller with his plans and obtains whatever additional details he can about the reasons for the conversion, he should have a meeting with all of his sales clerks and inform them of the plans and the reasons for it. They should know as soon as possible. They will no doubt get wind that something is about to happen and then start speculating on it, which is far worse than knowing the actual truth. The supervisor should certainly anticipate that the employees are going to be shocked and unhappy over the news. He has no other jobs to offer the 20 who will be terminated, and, in fact, he has no alternative but to tell them the facts.

Although he may have in mind five employees who he believes would make the best cashiers, he should not reveal his choices when he holds his initial meeting with them. He should merely say that five employees will be required for training as cashiers. He should tell them as much as he knows about the duties of the cashier jobs and ask those who believe they would be interested to let him know. This is a safer approach than picking the cashiers he wants in advance. Not all of the five chosen might be interested in the job. Some of the others might be interested, but they might be offended because they were not chosen in the first place. He might give all of those who express an interest a short trial period, requiring them to check out a heavy volume of merchandise on the cash register. The five he finally selects should be the ones who demonstrate the most aptitude, speed, and accuracy.

He should make the selection as soon as possible to avoid keeping in suspense both those employees who will be retrained and those who will be terminated. The supervisor should anticipate that some of the employees will begin immediately looking for other jobs and will quit before the effective date of the conversion. He might be quite short-staffed before the conversion date, but he should accept this inconvenience as a small price to pay for the successful relocation of the displaced employees.

In a way, a technological change of this kind is the easiest to handle if the supervisor approaches it forth-

rightly. It is clear-cut. The change will occur on a specified date. The supervisor has no choice but to terminate
the employees whose jobs will be eliminated. He recognizes that the employees who are terminated will not like
it, but he will try to deal with them as fairly and as honestly as he can.

A supervisor could have created greater anxiety on
the part of all employees if he had handled this case in an
evasive manner. For example, after making his decision
regarding the number of cashiers to retain and after determining whom to keep and whom to terminate, he
might not have said anything to the employees until the
day before the effective date of the conversion. Or he
could have talked individually only to the five employees
he wanted to retain and asked them to say nothing to the
rest of the employees. His reasons for not discussing the
matter with the rest of the employees might have been
twofold. He might have been afraid that they would be
disturbed and unproductive for the 30 days leading to the
conversion date, and he might have wanted to avoid facing them with the bad news as long as possible. Then, too,
he might have been afraid that some of them would quit
before the end of the 30-day period, leaving him short-
staffed. So he went ahead with the physical changes in the
store but gave the employees no explanation of the reasons for them.

It is not difficult to speculate on the situation that
would have prevailed in the store during the 30-day period
if the supervisor had handled the problem in this way.
The employees soon would have known that some drastic
change was in the offing, and they might have known what
it was. An employee might accidentally have seen the
controller's telegram or overheard the telephone conversation between him and the supervisor. If not, one of the

workmen installing the cashier stands would surely have told them. The store would have been rife with speculation when the five chosen cashiers were individually called into the manager's office. When these employees also were evasive about their conversation with the manager, the rest of the clerks would most probably have guessed what had happened. Added to their acute anxiety would have been a growing hostility toward the manager and the firm for not being more frank with them.

A supervisor can always do a more effective job of handling change with his employees if he accepts it himself. In this case, if the manager had resisted the change, or if he had tried to persuade the controller not to terminate the excess sales clerks, it would have been more difficult for him to handle the situation smoothly.

The approach suggested in this instance seems best whenever technological change results in the elimination of jobs and there is no practical way of absorbing the displaced employees in other work. The issue should be faced squarely and speedily. Nothing is to be gained by evading the problem or by procrastinating. To use another example, suppose a restaurant employed a full-time butcher to cut and dress meats. The restaurant supervisor decided that it would be much more economical to buy ready-cut meats, thus eliminating the butcher's job. There would be no practical way for the supervisor to use the butcher in some other job. There is no point in suggesting that he be retrained as a cook, for example; he already is a skilled craftsman. Nor could the job be eliminated by normal attrition, unless the supervisor knows that the butcher is planning to leave anyway. The butcher should be told exactly what the situation is and the reasons for the change. Then he should be terminated. He should be given adequate separation pay and helped as much as possible to find another job.

Retraining

The store manager would have handled the situation differently if the controller's telegram had said the firm was opening several new stores in nearby areas and was switching to self-service in the interests of economy and better use of personnel. All present personnel who were interested would be retrained as cashiers for both the present store and the new ones planned. The manager's concern then would have been to find out which employees would be available to work in the new locations and then to start retraining them.

Many of the sales clerks no doubt could have performed well as cashiers, but some might not have. The two jobs require quite different skills. A pleasing approach and enthusiasm for the merchandise are far more important in selling than in cashiering jobs. Speed and accuracy in handling figures and money, often under pressure of heavy volume and impatient customers, are the prime requisites of cashiering work.

An unfortunate aspect of technological change is that many of the employees displaced when jobs are eliminated do not have the skills or aptitudes for new jobs. Supervisors need to be objective and realistic about the abilities of their employees and the requirements of new jobs. They have a responsibility to management to see that jobs are filled with the most competent people possible. They should not be swayed by their sympathies and a desire to help an employee who does not have what it takes to perform the new work. Retraining efforts should be focused on those employees who have demonstrated the interest and ability to learn the new work and to perform it satisfactorily.

The supervisor's responsibility extends only to retraining employees for jobs that are under his control. It is not his function to give a displaced employee vocational guidance or to determine what kind of work he might be trained for. There are public agencies, such as the local office of the state employment service, that are much better equipped to counsel the employee. In a large organization, displaced employees might be absorbed into jobs in other departments. The supervisor should work closely with his personnel office and with other supervisors in attempting to relocate his employees.

Making Technology Serve the Supervisor

Technological advance can and should be a boon to the supervisor. It can relieve him of detailed surveillance of routine activities and permit him to concentrate on the more creative aspects of his job. The variety store manager probably spent the major part of his time supervising and training the 25 sales clerks. Once the five cashiers were fully trained, they would need little day-to-day supervision because automatic controls could be established over their jobs. The manager could then devote his major efforts to improved merchandising. He could experiment with various displays and promotional schemes. He could analyze the turnover of different items and then weed out dead or slow-moving items and push the good sellers. He would have an opportunity to increase the sales and the earnings of the store.

Conversion of routine clerical work to the computer should offer the same advantage. Very often it does not. The conversion itself is often painful, with errors and omissions creating havoc with the records. Supervisors who are familiar with the work itself often know nothing about computer operations, while the computer systems analysts and programmers do not understand the work. For this reason, systems and programs are often incorrect or missing in important details. Moreover, the manual procedure might have been cumbersome; full of duplications, omissions, and inconsistencies; and held together by a clerk who was so familiar with the procedure that she could check and double-check and pick up errors. This chaotic procedure might have been programmed as is into the computer, thereby perpetuating and compounding its weaknesses.

The technical competence of a supervisor should stand him in good stead at the time of technological change. His intimate knowledge of the work and his ability to visualize its many elements as well as the finished product should permit him to iron out problems and to provide systems analysts with crucial details. Before the conversion begins, the supervisor should familiarize himself as much as possible with computer operations by talking to the computer people and working closely with them during the planning stages.

Supervisors often resist technological change themselves because they see it as a threat. They are afraid that once they are relieved of details, they will be expected to do a creative job that they might not be capable of doing. The variety store manager might have resisted the change to self-service if he was afraid he *would* be expected to improve merchandising methods or increase sales and if he doubted his ability to do that. An accountant might resist having much of the accounting work put onto a computer because he is afraid of the kind of job he will have once he is relieved of detail. He might fear that he is not qualified to do the financial analysis and forecasting that might be demanded of him. In a time of rapid change, it is imperative that supervisors continue to grow and learn. They cannot afford to lose their skills or knowledge through lack of use.

Obsolescence of Skills and Training

It is nearly impossible to think of a skill or a kind of training that remains static in today's world. Training and learning no longer end when a person completes his formal education. An engineer, for all intents and purposes, ceases being an engineer if he fails to keep abreast of developments in his field. Physicians and nurses are not equipped to practice without refresher training if they drop out of their fields for a few years. All of the scientific professions are in a state of rapid and continual change. Skilled and semiskilled work is very much the same. Perhaps one of the most static occupations is routine clerical work, and that is the most susceptible to automation.

Supervisors have a double responsibility for keeping skills and training from becoming out of date. They need to stimulate their employees to continue learning and studying and keeping their skills up through practice. They also need to make sure that their own skills and training do not become obsolete. If they do become obsolete through technological change, the supervisors need to have the flexibility and motivation to learn something new.

Changing Work Methods and Procedures

Supervisors are frequently required to make other changes which have far less impact than the elimination of the job. They may want to introduce new methods or new procedures that will simplify and speed up the work. They may encounter the same kind of resistance from employees to these changes, even though there is no threat whatever to the job itself.

This kind of resistance to change has interested social scientists for many years. Two scientists, Lester Coch and John R. P. French,[1] conducted a study in a clothing factory to observe the phenomenon. They worked with different groups of operators during the introduction of a change in the work procedure. The groups were about equal in efficiency ratings and cohesiveness, and the work change would have approximately the same effect on each group. The change was introduced to the first group by a *no-participation* method. The operators were called into a room and were told by staff people that there was a need for a slight change in the work procedure. They were told in detail what the change would be and the reasons for it. They were then sent back to work, using the new method.

The change was introduced to two other groups on what the researchers called a *total-participation* basis. The total-participation groups met with the staff men, who dramatically demonstrated to them the need for cost reduction. The staff men and the operators agreed that some savings could be effected. The groups then discussed how current work methods could be improved and unnecessary operations eliminated. They agreed on new work methods, which the operators were then trained to use.

The study showed that there was a remarkable difference between the output rate of the no-participation group and the two total-participation groups. The output of the no-participation group dropped immediately to about two-

[1] "Overcoming Resistance to Change," *Human Relations,* Vol. 1, No. 4, 1948.

thirds of its former rate and remained at this level during the 30-day period while the change was being introduced. Resistance developed immediately; there were marked expressions of aggression toward management, conflict with the methods engineer, and hostility toward the supervisor. There was a deliberate restriction of production and a lack of cooperation. Some of the operators quit; others filed grievances.

The total-participation groups showed a smaller initial drop in output at the beginning of the change, but they made a rapid recovery to a rate that exceeded the previous rate under the old method. There were no signs of hostility in these groups toward the methods engineer or the supervisor.

As expected, the researchers concluded that resistance to change could be overcome by having employees actively participate in making the change.

Paul R. Lawrence provides an interesting view of this interpretation of the Coch and French study based on his own observations regarding resistance to change.[2] Lawrence observed the reaction of a factory operator to suggested work changes made by two different industrial engineers. In the first situation, the operator had been assigned to work with the engineer on assembling and testing an experimental product that the engineer was developing. The two individuals were in almost constant contact in their work. There was an easy give-and-take between the two of them in suggesting and trying out new ideas. The engineer would suggest an idea, discuss it with the operator, and ask her to try it out. Or she would get an idea and pass it on to the engineer, who would consider

[2] "How to Deal with Resistance to Change," in Edward C. Bursk (editor), *Human Relations for Management,* Harper & Brothers, N.Y., 1956.

it and possibly ask her to try it out. There was no resistance to change on the part of the operator to any new ideas or methods.

Lawrence then observed the reaction of the same operator when she was approached by a different industrial engineer and asked to try out a new part. The engineer walked up to her and indicated by a gesture that he wanted her to assemble some units with the new part. She picked up one of the parts and started to assemble it, but she did not handle it with her usual care. She then tested it, and it failed to pass inspection. She triumphantly told the engineer that the part did not work. When she tried another part given her by the same engineer, the same process was repeated all over again. None of them worked.

Lawrence concluded from these observations that the interpersonal relationship between the operator and the engineer was the key to her resistance or lack of resistance to new methods or ideas. The first engineer treated the operator as a person with valuable skills and knowledge, even when he approached her with a new idea. When the second engineer approached her, however, his lack of any explanation and his brusque manner led her to believe that her customary work relationship was being changed, and she responded unfavorably to the way he was treating her.

The results in the Coch and French study can be explained in the same way, according to Lawrence. The company's personnel policies were progressive, and a high value was placed on fair and open dealings with employees. Yet management did not follow this customary treatment when it simply brought the no-participation group into the room and told them of the change. On this occasion, the operators were treated as if they had no useful knowledge and were not the skilled and efficient operators that they thought they were. On top of that, a methods engineer had decided how they should do their job. They interpreted this treatment as a threatening change in their relationship with management and their supervisor.

On the other hand, the two total-participation groups were treated in accordance with the customary relationship between them and management. They attached no great significance to the new method since they were treated in their usual way. Their suggestions and ideas were asked for, and they saw nothing threatening in the change.

The relationship between the supervisor and an employee has an undeniable effect on the employee's receptivity to new work methods. If the supervisor treats the employee as if he respects his ideas and skill, if he frequently asks the employee for suggestions, work improvements may be accepted as a matter of course. But if the supervisor habitually treats the employee as if he had no ideas of his own, if he merely tells the employee what to do and never asks for his opinions, then the supervisor will probably fail if he suddenly attempts to have the employee participate in trying out a new work method. Participation is not something that can be turned on and off at will. It is not a technique; it is a continuing relationship between the supervisor and the employee.

This does not imply that overcoming resistance to change is simply a matter of treating employees as skilled, intelligent individuals who have valuable knowledge. Some resistance is inevitable. Employees at times cannot see any purpose or advantage to a proposed change in work method. It makes no sense to them. They are unable to visualize the end result, or they have ungrounded fears of what might happen.

In such a case, the supervisor should not permit the

employees' resistance to deter him from making a needed change. He should try to find out what is troubling the employees. Some resistance might be based on their knowledge of details that he is unaware of or has overlooked. It is important to distinguish between resistance that is based on fact and reason and resistance that is based on fantasy or lack of understanding. When supervisors fail to make this distinction, they may blindly forge ahead with a new plan that is unworkable and will fail. However, if the supervisor is convinced that his plan is sound and will work, he should move forward with it, working closely with the employees until the change is accomplished. It sometimes happens that employees who strenuously resist a new idea will become its ardent advocates once they see that it improves the job.

A supervisor can introduce changes more readily if he has established a climate that is conducive to new ideas and growth. If all employees are expected to suggest ways for improving the work, the introduction of new methods may be accepted as routine.

12

The Leadership Challenge

THE SUPERVISOR HAS A DEMANDING ROLE. HE must have a variety of skills, both conceptual and interpersonal. He must have good judgment in sizing up situations and people. He must have the courage to tackle unpleasant tasks and to make decisions and take actions that may not be popular. He must be able to adapt his behavior to varying circumstances and to different personalities.

Leadership is a very difficult quality to define because it may mean different things under different circumstances. In the supervisor's case, it is the composite of all the qualities just mentioned. It is supervisory behavior that stimulates employees to achieve, to do their best, and to want to do more. It cannot exist apart from the personalities of both the leader and those led. Behavior that becomes leadership of one group in one situation may not be leadership of another group in another situation. Leading troops in battle may be quite different from leading a group of women clerks. Leading a football team is different from leading a group of highly trained scientists.

Leadership contains at least three essential ingredients: (1) rapport between the leader and those led, (2) behavior that adapts appropriately to circumstances, and (3) mutual confidence and trust between the leader and the led.

Employees as a Group

In order to be a good leader, a supervisor must know the personalities and abilities of each individual under him. He must anticipate their possible reactions to different approaches. He must also understand his employees as a group and anticipate the *group* reaction to new plans, changes, and policies. He must decide when it is best to deal with his employees individually and when to work with them as a group.

All kinds of forces and pressures operate on individuals when they become members of a group. A supervisor may have a discussion with an individual employee to explain some changes in work methods that he wants to try. The changes affect only the job of this one employee. The employee reacts quite favorably to his ideas and is eager to try them. She leaves the interview and tells her co-workers of the new plans. They may suggest to her various reasons for the plan to fail. They may convince her that the supervisor's *real* intent is to do away with her job and that she is being naïve to go along with it. The employee may become more and more upset by the opinions of her co-workers and may finally decide that she will resist the changes as strongly as possible. When the unsuspecting supervisor approaches her with the first change for her to try out, he is surprised to see the difference in her attitude. She is now convinced that the plan will not succeed.

There may be several reasons for the group to have behaved as it did and for the employee to have been as strongly influenced as she was by the group pressure. There may be a lack of trust between the supervisor and his employees. Perhaps the group, or some members of it, are really suspicious of his intentions. Or this individual employee may be so impressionable and easily influenced that the group enjoys the sport of getting her upset and controlling her opinions. She may be so unsure of herself and her relations with the supervisor that she is ready to believe the worst about anything. Whatever the reason, the pressures operating on the employee from within the group can make things very difficult for the supervisor and can have a tremendous influence on the way he manages his unit. Perhaps he needs to give this individual employee stronger and more direct supervision to build her self-confidence and to counter the influence of the group. Perhaps he needs to find out which member of the group is having the most negative influence and isolate that person by giving him a different assignment that will take him out of close working relations with other employees. The appropriate action for the supervisor to take will depend on his assessment of the pressures and the individuals.

Members of a group have varying degrees of influence. Some lead while others follow. Some may have a positive influence; others may have a negative influence. Some may play different roles at different times. One day they lead, and the next day they follow. Leadership of a group often is not static; it ebbs and flows.

Individuals may play different roles in combination with each other. One or two members may team up to espouse a certain point of view. A member who is usually reticent about expressing his views may assume leadership if another employee whom he admires supports his position. Another individual may always follow the lead of a particular employee. Much of the activity that goes on in the work group is perfectly harmless. It is only when the group pressures begin to have an adverse effect on the work that the supervisor should intervene.

When certain members of a group invariably influence the other members negatively, the supervisor has to take some kind of action. If he fails to do so, the group (or the dominant members of it) may successfully challenge his authority to manage the unit. Very often a new supervisor who takes charge of a unit may find that everything he tries to do runs into trouble and that it is virtually impossible for him to get the group to accept his supervision. He needs to learn as much as possible about each individual in the group and the effects all the different employees are having on each other. He may eventually find that one member is having a subversive influence on the others. The supervisor will have to learn as best he can the reasons for the behavior of this individual. He may be able to win over the subversive leader, but this is doubtful. For whatever reason, this employee wants to challenge the authority of the supervisor. The supervisor may have to force a showdown with him and either transfer him out of the unit or discharge him. Drastic action of this sort may be the only way the supervisor can gain the respect of the other employees under him. If he fails to act, or if he passively submits to the employee leader or attempts to negotiate with him things that are not negotiable, he will never be able to exert authority over the group.

Some employees are so impressionable that they are influenced, either positively or negatively, by any person with whom they work. The supervisor must be sure that such an employee is teamed with another, stronger person who can exert a favorable influence on him. The supervisor may need to devote particular efforts himself to an employee of this personality in order to help him gain self-confidence and a willingness to stand on his own feet.

Not all group pressures are negative, of course. When teamwork and close coordination are required among various employees, the supervisor wants a cohesive group that communicates easily. In this case, he should work—at least in part—with the employees as a group. He should hold staff meetings of the group to discuss new plans or ideas and to stimulate the group to think of ways of improving the work. If he establishes a climate of free and open communication and puts a premium on suggestions for new ideas and improvements, the supervisor may well find that the group serves as a stimulus to the individual members. The supervisor should encourage the group members to discuss the work with each other, to iron out problems, and to think of better ways of doing the job. The relaxed give-and-take of the group can provide a good environment for trying out new ideas suggested by various members. Employees may be more likely to suggest new methods to the group than they would be to submit them to the supervisor.

However, the supervisor must keep in close touch with each member of the group. He must treat them as individuals, each with skills, knowledge, and ideas. He should not designate certain employees to act as leaders of the group and then work only with or through those individuals. Nor should he assume that certain employees are the natural leaders and work only with or through them or look to them as group spokesmen. He must stimulate each person to contribute as much as possible and assume as much responsibility as he can.

The Supervisor as Management Representative

A supervisor is a part of management. He has a definite obligation to carry out the policies and plans of upper-level management and to run his unit in the way that will contribute the most to the objectives of the organization.

As a management representative, he must keep his employees informed of management policies and decisions. He should explain and interpret these policies and decisions to them. If a new method or program is decided upon by management, the supervisor has an obligation to introduce it to his employees in such a way that they will see the reasons for it. And he should work with them in getting the change accepted.

Occasionally, a supervisor will respond to the group pressures of his subordinates in the same way that an individual employee responds to pressures from co-workers. A member of management may discuss a new method or plan with a supervisor. The supervisor may agree to it enthusiastically and go back to tell his employees about it. They may suggest a dozen reasons for the failure of the plan. They may fear all kinds of adverse effects from it, and they may convince the supervisor that the plan is bad and should be rejected. He may then go back to management and say that he has decided the plan cannot work. Or he may develop the kind of resistance that we have previously discussed and, without saying anything to management, just not implement the change. In such a case, the supervisor has failed to carry out his obligations. He is responsible for leading his employees, not following them or letting them lead him. Of course, if his employees had pointed out valid procedural defects, the supervisor should have taken them into account and modified the plan to correct them.

The supervisor should serve as a true link between his employees and upper levels of management. He must also interpret to management the problems and attitudes of his employees. He should let his own superior know how his employees are progressing and should inform him when they have done an outstanding job or have accomplished something significant.

Predicting Supervisory Success

Is there any way to identify those characteristics of personality or performance in a potential supervisor that will help predict his chances of success? Can we observe an individual working in a nonsupervisory capacity and say with any confidence that he would make a good supervisor? If it were possible, many problems of weak or deficient supervision might be avoided. Unfortunately, such prediction is very difficult because we cannot observe a person's behavior under the same circumstances that would obtain if he were a supervisor.

We might be able to suggest some clues to supervisory performance, however. To be a good supervisor, a person certainly must be able to relate to people and must enjoy working with them. But here we must be careful, because the gregarious, outgoing person who gets along well with people and who is well liked is the one most often selected for a supervisory job, and he may be the most likely to fail. Everything depends upon *how* he works with people.

If he is perceptive and aware of people's reactions and feelings, if he has a somewhat analytical interest in people's responses to various situations, if he enjoys working with people to *solve problems,* and if he enjoys the challenge of introducing new ideas and getting them accepted, he may have the qualities that would make a good supervisor. But, if his getting along with people means submitting to their views or evading any issues that might lead to conflict, if he avoids taking any stands that might be unpopular, if he goes along with anything, if he wants more than anything else to be liked, he should not be put in a supervisory job. Perhaps *problem solving* is the key to the difference. A good supervisor must have the ability to work effectively with people in solving problems.

An individual who is withdrawn, extremely shy, or ill at ease with people should not be a supervisor. He would probably shut himself up in his office and avoid any contact with his employees. As for the individual who has spent years working alone on a research project or in a job involving detail, the chances are very poor for supervisory success with this kind of person. He apparently enjoys the type of work environment he has been in for many years, an environment where he is completely attuned to *things* rather than to *people.* He may be unaware of and uninterested in the responses and emotions of people, and he would find it impossible to cope with them.

Of course, a person must also have something of an analytical mind to be a good supervisor. He must be able to relate to the *work* as well as to his employees. He must be able to see ways of improving work and work methods.

A willingness to stand up for what he thinks is right is certainly an essential quality. A supervisor often has to take unpopular stands and stick to them. But he also has to be flexible enough to know when to compromise, when to stand firm, and when to retreat or delay. Judgment is an indispensable ingredient here, as is the ability to communicate his ideas and views and to get people to accept them.

It has been suggested that any potential supervisor should be required to serve a trial period or in internship before he is finally appointed. This plan may have merit, but it also may be worthless. A person could serve in a supervisory position for a year or more without having to face any of the really hard problems in supervision. To be at all useful, the trial period would have to be structured carefully and rather scientifically in order to provide a variety of experiences that are typical of the supervisory job and that would be a valid test of the potential supervisor's judgment and skill. Furthermore, it would be necessary to devise an objective means of observing the trainee's responses to the various situations and measuring the level of his performance.

Because of its challenge, because of the variety and complexity of problems that have to be faced and solved, and because of its tremendous opportunity for innovation and creativity, supervision is a dynamic and fascinating undertaking.

Index

271

hospital (*continued*)
    preadmission information for, 99
    technological change and, 240
hotel chambermaid, job structure of, 41–45
human relations:
    skill in, 31–32
    Mayo's work in, 128
hygienic factors, job attitudes and, 58–61

individual employee:
    coordinating work of, 37
    vs. group, 261–265
    see also employee
individual growth, job structure and, 49
instruction:
    follow-up on, 116
    nature of, 117
    wrong kind of, 118
interpersonal friction, 165–166
interpersonal skills, of supervisor, 29–32
interview:
    controlling and ending of, 205
    evaluating information of, 206
    listening in, 202
    personal nature of, 197–208
    primary purpose of, 204
    questions in, 202–203
    stereotypes of, 207
    verification in, 208–209

job:
    dynamic vs. static, 64–65
    educational and experience requirements of, 67
    "good feeling" about, 57–58
    as motivation in itself, 60
    motivators vs. hygienic factors in, 58–61
    overspecializing of, 44
    see also job enrichment; job evaluation; work
job applicant, interview of, 197–209

About the Author

Since 1966 MAXINE BISHOP has been chief of employee development for the Bureau of Labor Statistics in Washington, D.C. Previous to joining the federal government, she was self-employed as a management consultant in San Francisco, California. Mrs. Bishop received bachelor's and master's degrees in business administration from the University of California at Berkeley.